UNSELLABLE

Build a business around your expertise.

One they can't buy, and you'd never want to sell.

STEVE CORNEY

CONTENTS

Acknowledgments	4
About The Author, Learn Awesome, Self-Sponsored & Unsellable	7
Preface: The Unsellable Business & The Self-Sponsored Revolution	14
How To Use This Book	19
PART I FOUNDATIONS	**23**
Chapter 1: You Are the Business	24
Chapter 2: The Self-Sponsored Expert Movement	31
Chapter 3: The 3 Must-Haves to Be In the Club	41
PART II THE ECOSYSTEM	**51**
Chapter 4: The Expert Ecosystem Flywheel	52
Chapter 5: Strategic Building: Choose, Pre-Sell, Then Build	65
Chapter 6: Your Tech Stack Can't Be Shit	75
PART III ACQUISITION & SALES	**87**
Chapter 7: Marketing That Doesn't Make You Hate Yourself	88
Chapter 8: The Two Funnels That Feed the Machine	100
Chapter 9: How to Price Like a Weaponised Genius	112
Chapter 10: Sales That Don't Feel Gross	124
Chapter 11: The PACER Sales Conversation Framework	133
PART IV PROTECTION & LIFESTYLE	**144**
Chapter 12: Living the Unsellable Life	145
Chapter 13: Protecting Your IP Without Paranoia	155
Chapter 14: The Mic Drop	166

ACKNOWLEDGMENTS

This book wouldn't exist without the people who shaped my journey, both those who are still here and those who live on in what they taught me.

To my dad, who left this world when I was just 12 but whose lessons remain with me every day. You showed me the importance of relationships, connecting with people, and solving problems. Those fundamentals have become the bedrock of everything I've built.

To my mum, whose sudden passing when I was 30 became both an ending and a beginning. You showed me what true love and sacrifice are all about. I built Learn Awesome in the wake of losing you, turning grief into purpose in a way I hope would make you proud.

To my brother Matt, the most exceptional role model for my niece. Your strength, commitment, and character show me what family truly means.

To Harps. Being your uncle is the most important role I'll ever play. You're the best and will shine so brightly in this world. You remind me daily why creating something meaningful matters.

To Paulie. Mentor, surrogate dad, great friend, and legal mind who showed me how to protect what matters while sharing what creates impact. Your guidance goes far beyond intellectual property law. You've shown me what it means to lead with generosity and wisdom. This book, and so much of my work, carries your influence on every page.

To my incredible team at Learn Awesome. You're all amazing. Your dedication, creativity, and commitment to our mission make it possible to create impact at scale. This book exists because you handle the details while I focus on the vision. Thank you for believing in what we're building together.

To my clients. Both the corporate partners who trust us with their people and the brilliant experts who trust us with their ideas. To our corporate clients: thank you for opening your doors to new thinking and being willing to transform how your people learn and grow. To our experts: your genius deserves to be seen, and your courage in sharing it inspires me daily. Special thanks to the founding members of the Expert Incubator who were willing to go first, test approaches, and help refine what would eventually become the Unsellable model.

And finally, to you, the reader. The expert who's picked up this book because something inside you knows there's a better way to build. You're not just in business; you're on a mission to transform how people think, work, and live. The world desperately needs your unique expertise, delivered in your authentic voice without compromise or dilution.

This book is my contribution to your journey. May it help you build something so perfectly aligned with who you are that you'd never dream of selling it, not because it isn't valuable, but because it's invaluable.

Here's to the experts who are changing the world, one unsellable business at a time.

Cheers,

ABOUT THE AUTHOR, LEARN AWESOME, SELF-SPONSORED & UNSELLABLE

FINDING MY PATH

I have always been a bit of a square peg in a round hole.

My mother made enormous sacrifices to ensure that I received an excellent education. She was still paying it off twelve years after I graduated. So I went to university, more for her than for myself. After all, good sons followed traditional paths. But even then, I knew that the traditional corporate ladder was not for me. I wasn't looking for fancy titles or corner offices. I just wanted to work on my terms, doing something that actually mattered.

This was not just stubborn independence. At 12 years old, I lost my dad. Suddenly, I had to teach myself all the things my friends were learning from their fathers. While they had built-in mentors, I was piecing together my education through trial, error, and sheer necessity.

That early experience forged a lifelong pattern: teaching myself whatever I needed to know and developing a deep appreciation for how people actually learn.

THE PLATE-SPINNER YEARS

After university, I landed one of my only "real jobs" as a trainer and facilitator. That gig was my introduction to corporate training. And I saw immediately how broken most of it was. Boring, generic, forgettable.

I started freelancing, running workshops, and building training programs for large Aussie companies. But being me, one focus was never enough. I was the ultimate plate spinner.

I bought and ran a gym. Then, I sold it to buy not one but two ice cream stores. Because apparently, running multiple physical businesses while freelancing was not challenging enough.

I was learning, building, experimenting. Trying to find where my skills and passions could create the most impact. What I did not realise then was how these physical businesses would teach me the hardest lesson of my life.

THE DAY EVERYTHING CHANGED

When my mum passed suddenly when I was 30, I was working at one of my ice cream stores. In the midst of that crushing grief came a brutal realisation: because my business had a door (literally), if I did not go back to work the very next day and scoop ice cream, I could not pay the rent. The business would fail.

That moment crystallised everything for me. On 1 December 2016, I made a commitment I have never broken: I would never again own a business that had a door. I would go all in on what would become Learn Awesome and build something that could work on my terms. High margin, location-independent, and completely self-sponsored.

With both parents gone, I had no safety net, no inheritance, no easy path forward. Just my ideas, my experience, and a stubborn belief that learning could be done better.

BUILDING THE BRIDGE

What drove me was a simple observation that had become increasingly clear after years in the training world: the gap between experts with transformative knowledge and the employees who desperately needed that knowledge was massive.

Companies were serving up cookie-cutter training programs created by algorithms and generic content mills. Employees were starving for real expertise. And brilliant experts were struggling to package and scale their knowledge.

I saw an opportunity to bridge that gap. To create a vehicle that would give experts access to employees and employees access to experts.

Learn Awesome became that bridge. We work with incredible experts to help them package their knowledge into powerful learning experiences. Then, we deliver those programs inside companies, meaning the experts' clients are our clients too.

I passionately believe that employees deserve access to the best knowledge, the best thought leadership, and the best programs in the world. Learn Awesome exists to make that happen. Designing and building e-learning and training solutions that create real, lasting impact.

THE CONNECTION AGENCY

Today, Learn Awesome is privileged to be the agency that connects these two worlds. We bring together brilliant experts with the companies that need their knowledge.

Our role is to package content in the most optimal way, ensuring experts' ideas translate into transformative learning experiences for corporate employees. We design, build, and implement solutions that serve both sides of this critical relationship.

It is an absolute privilege to facilitate these connections. To help experts monetise their genius while giving companies access to the best thinking in the world. Being the trusted partner that makes these relationships successful is a responsibility we take seriously every day.

NO DOORS, JUST IMPACT

Today, Learn Awesome allows me to work from anywhere in the world with just my laptop and an internet connection. One day, I might be helping an expert launch their program from a beachside café. The next, I am facilitating a client workshop from a completely different time zone.

My entire team works remotely too, because geographic flexibility is one of our core values. We have deliberately built a business with no doors. Just the ability to do what we love and impact others from wherever we choose to be.

This is not just a nice lifestyle perk. It is proof that the model works. When you build an expert business the right way, your income is not tied to a location, your impact is not limited by your working hours, and your growth is not capped by your personal capacity.

TRULY UNSELLABLE

Here is the thing about Learn Awesome. While it is a brand name, it is literally an extension of me. It is not designed to be packaged up and flogged off to the highest bidder someday.

When Learn Awesome is finished and we do not want to do it anymore, there is no 10x or 20x exit waiting. I might get a few bucks for my second-hand laptop on Marketplace, but that was never the point.

The point was to create a vehicle that allows and affords me and my team the chance to live our lives doing the work and the things we love. A business that serves us, not the other way around.

You can do the same. This book is the extension and expression of how to do this. A blueprint for creating something so aligned with who you are that selling it would feel like selling a piece of yourself.

WHY THIS MATTERS

Here is what I have learned: your expertise is not just valuable. It is bloody essential.

There are employees right now, sitting in companies, desperate for what you know. Not the watered-down, corporate-approved version. The real, experienced, battle-tested wisdom that only comes from someone who has lived it.

The old model keeps you separate from those people. It puts intermediaries, platforms, and systems between you and the humans who need what you know.

The Unsellable model removes those barriers. It packages your expertise in a way that lets it travel directly to the people who need it. While making sure you get paid what you are worth.

That is what this book is about. Not just business strategy. Not just packaging. Not just sales.

It is about creating a direct line between your genius and the people who need it. And building a business that serves your life, not the other way around.

WELCOME TO THE MOVEMENT

I am not here to sell you a dream. I am here to show you a path I have walked. And helped hundreds of others walk.

It is not easy. It is not automatic. But it is possible.

Welcome to Self-Sponsored. Welcome to becoming Unsellable.

I am genuinely chuffed that Learn Awesome, my team, and I get to show you the way and support you on this journey.

Because the world needs your expertise delivered your way and on your terms.

It is time to build something so perfectly aligned with who you are that you would never want to sell it. Not because it is not valuable but because it is invaluable.

Let's get started.

PREFACE:
THE UNSELLABLE BUSINESS & THE SELF-SPONSORED REVOLUTION

A DIFFERENT KIND OF BUSINESS

Y ou were never meant to build a business to sell.

You were meant to build a business that lets you live. Really live. On your terms. With your rules. Powered by your ideas.

This is not a book about building an empire. This is a book about building a practice, a purpose-led, high-margin, expert-powered machine that gives you options, autonomy, and impact without sacrificing your time, energy, or soul.

It's about becoming unsellable, not because your business isn't valuable, but because it's too valuable to give away. And it's about doing it all while being self-sponsored: No VC. No grants. No gatekeepers. Just you, your IP, a laptop, and a fire in your gut to do meaningful work for the people who need it most.

THE B2B FOCUS

Let me be upfront: this book primarily focuses on selling your expertise to businesses rather than individuals. Why? Because it's more efficient and more lucrative.

Think about it: to sell 1,000 seats of your program to individuals, you'd need 1,000 separate conversations and sales processes. With what I call the 1:many:1 strategy, you can sell 1,000 seats to 1,000 employees by talking to just one decision-maker.

That doesn't mean B2C models don't work. They absolutely can. However, building a B2B foundation first gives you stability, scale, and higher margins. Plus, once you have B2B offerings, you can easily adapt them for individual consumers. The reverse path is much harder.

So, while the principles in this book apply to any expertise-based business, our primary focus is on positioning yourself to solve problems that companies recognise, value, and budget for.

THE BROKEN PLAYBOOK

Let's be honest about where we are. The traditional expert playbook isn't just outdated. It's broken.

Coaches are burning out trying to scale. Consultants are undercharging for transformative work. Keynote speakers are crushing it on stage and then crumbling when someone asks, "So how can we work with you?"

Everyone's chasing the same nonsense:

- Building funnels that look like everyone else's
- Creating "passive income" that requires active hustle
- Scaling through teams that eat all your profit
- Designing businesses that strip away what makes you valuable

This book is the new playbook. It's not theory. It's not hope. It's a battle-tested system for experts who are tired of playing by rules that weren't designed for them.

WHO THIS IS FOR

This is for the experts who are already being paid but not yet being paid properly. It's for the ones who know they're brilliant but don't have the ecosystem to back it up.

It's for the legends doing one-to-one or one-to-many but haven't figured out how to have their ideas keep working even when they're not in the room.

This is a field guide for experts who want to make a dent, without needing a team of 20 or a $50k funnel.

And let's be clear: this is going to take work. Real work. Strategic work. But it's work that actually pays off instead of just keeping you busy.

THE UNSELLABLE MODEL

We're building a business that isn't trying to exit. We're building a business that:

- Solves real problems for employees in big companies
- Builds assets around your ideas, not your time
- Has multiple ways to work with you
- Is lean, scalable, and insanely profitable
- Doesn't rely on you being available 24/7
- And gives you the freedom to surf, write, speak, coach, or just breathe

This isn't about diminishing your ambition. It's about focusing it where it matters, creating something so perfectly aligned with who you are that selling it would feel like selling a piece of yourself.

Could you sell it? Absolutely. Will you want to? Not a chance. That's the power of building unsellable.

THE SELF-SPONSORED PHILOSOPHY

I built Learn Awesome from nothing. No loans. No seed funding. No magic mentor. Just me, my IP, and the drive to help people learn better.

Over 17 years later, I've helped experts sell their ideas to companies, build eLearns that scale, and license programs to clients who fund the development before they're even built.

This book is the essence of everything I've learned, including the failures and dead ends. It's raw. It's unfiltered. It's tested.

It's for people who want to live on purpose and get paid damn well for doing what they're brilliant at.

WHAT YOU'RE ABOUT TO LEARN

This book isn't just inspiration. It's a blueprint. A system.

A machine you can build.

You'll learn:

- How to package your genius into scalable, leverageable formats
- How to build a flywheel of offerings that feed each other
- How to price based on value, not time
- How to sell without feeling like a used car salesman
- How to protect your IP without paranoia
- How to build tech that works for you, not against you
- How to market yourself without losing your soul

All of it centered around you, your expertise, your voice, and your unique way of solving problems.

THE MOVEMENT BEGINS HERE

If you're ready to stop playing small... If you're tired of trading time for money... If you know you're worth more than you're charging...

Welcome to the movement.

Let's burn the old rules. Let's build something unsellable.

HOW TO USE
THIS BOOK

This book is organised to guide you through a complete system for transforming your expertise into a sustainable, high-margin business. Here's how to get the most from it:

THE BOOK'S STRUCTURE

PART I: FOUNDATIONS Chapters 1-3: The core principles of the Unsellable approach and whether this model is right for you.

PART II: THE ECOSYSTEM Chapters 4-6: How to build your Expert Ecosystem Flywheel and create the infrastructure to support it.

PART III: ACQUISITION & SALES Chapters 7-11: Marketing, sales, and pricing strategies that attract ideal clients without compromising your values.

PART IV: PROTECTION & LIFESTYLE Chapters 12-13: How to secure your intellectual property and design a business that serves your life goals.

THE IMPLEMENTATION APPROACH

Unlike most business books that overwhelm you with endless action items, I'm not here to create a massive to-do list that sits untouched. I'm here to create real change in your approach to your expertise business.

This is a marathon, not a sprint.

Each chapter ends with three focused actions:

- **ONE BIG THING**: The single most important action that will move the needle
- **Two Small Steps**: Quick wins you can implement with minimal time investment

Focus on implementing the ONE BIG THING from each chapter before moving to the next. The small steps are there for momentum, but the big thing is where transformation happens.

Remember, there's an entire ecosystem of resources waiting for you through Learn Awesome and the Expert Incubator when you're ready to go deeper on any particular aspect.

After reading about the Expert Ecosystem in Part II, you'll be invited to take the Expert Readiness Diagnostic. This will be your ONE BIG THING for that chapter and will help you identify exactly where to focus your implementation efforts.

NAVIGATION TIPS

1. **Read in Order First**: Work through the book from start to finish on your first read. Fold corners or use bookmarks to flag chapters you want to revisit.

2. **Start with the Assessment**: Chapter 3 contains the three must-haves to determine if you're ready for this model.

3. **Use the Case Studies**: Real-world examples show how others have applied these principles to overcome specific challenges.

4. **Build Iteratively**: You don't need to implement everything at once. Choose what addresses your most pressing needs first.

A QUICK WORD ABOUT THE CASE STUDIES IN THIS BOOK

Let's be real: you are probably thinking, "Yeah, sure, Steve. More made-up case studies to sell a book."

But every expert here is real. Every result is real. Every transformation is real.

The only thing I have changed is their names because these experts work with real corporate clients who pay real money. They don't need their IP, client relationships, or commercial arrangements plastered all over a book for the world to see.

The successes are theirs. The results are theirs. The systems they've built are theirs.

If you want the unfiltered version with names, faces, and all the details? That's what the Expert Incubator is for. That's where you'll meet these legends in person, see their work up close, and learn directly from their journey.

This book isn't about them, though. It's about you. It's about giving you the blueprint to build your own Unsellable business without compromising who you are or what you stand for.

So, as you read these case studies, know that these aren't feel-good fairy tales. They're documented proof that the system works if you're willing to put in the work.

AUDIO INSIGHTS

Throughout this book, you'll find QR codes at the end of each chapter marked with

🎧 BEYOND THE PAGE

These aren't audiobook snippets. They're chapter-specific audio insights where I share unfiltered implementation strategies and real-world applications for what you've just read. Each 2-3 minute audio provides deeper context and insider tips on applying that chapter's specific principles to your expertise business.

PART

FOUNDATIONS

"Your expertise isn't just what you do. It's who you are. The foundation of an unsellable business isn't a product or service, but the unique lens through which you see the world."

CHAPTER 1:

YOU ARE
THE BUSINESS

The Expert's Paradox
"You're not building a business.
You are the bloody business.
The day you stop apologising for
that is the day you start making
real money."

THE ESSENTIALS

- You are the business. Stop pretending you're not.
- Scale doesn't mean remove yourself, it means support yourself.
- An unsellable business is the most powerful business you can build.
- Most expert businesses break because they have no system or no soul.
- Building around your unique expertise isn't limiting, it's liberating.

CASE STUDY: SARAH - THE INVISIBLE EXPERT

BEFORE: Sarah had the brand, systems, and income but felt disconnected from her work. Her marketing sounded corporate. Her delivery felt hollow. She barely recognised herself in her own business.

ACTION: Sarah embraced the Unsellable model, rebuilding her business around her true voice: raw, direct, and provocative.

AFTER:

- Doubled her prices
- Expanded her client list
- Fell back in love with her work

"Turns out, I didn't need to build something separate from me. I needed to build something only I could create."

Let's be clear from the first line: **You're not building a business. You are the business.**

This isn't some hustle-porn, grind-til-you-die bullshit. This is about building something around you, your knowledge, your lived experience, your brilliance, and doing it in a way that's clean, profitable, and high-impact.

You don't need a 10-year exit strategy. You don't need to "scale" in a way that strips you out of the thing. And you sure as hell don't need to hide behind some brand name that sounds like a management consultancy from 1994.

What you need is a system, a way to make your work deliver value at scale without selling your soul in the process.

Because here's the truth most business books won't tell you:

You can build a business that's lean, highly profitable, and 100% aligned with who you are, and it can be "unsellable" by design.

Unsellable because it's built around your name. Unsellable because the value comes from your IP, your presence, and your unique sauce. Unsellable because no one can do it quite like you.

And that's not a weakness. That's the advantage.

THE ANATOMY OF AN EXPERT BUSINESS

If you're reading this, chances are:

- You've been paid for your knowledge
- You've delivered value to real people
- You've already got a book, a talk, a workshop, or a body of work that you're proud of

But here's what you probably don't have yet: A system that lets all those things work together.

Instead, you're stuck in the game most experts play:

- A few big months, followed by a dry patch
- A keynote here, a workshop there
- Clients saying, "How can we work with you?" and you freezing like a deer in the headlights

You know your shit. That's not the problem. The problem is you're trying to run a business instead of being "the" business.

THE TRADITIONAL MODEL VS. THE UNSELLABLE MODEL

The traditional business model demands that you:

- Build something separate from yourself
- Create systems that remove you from the equation
- Focus on "exit potential" above all else
- Scale by hiring, not by leveraging

But for true experts, this approach destroys the very value you've created.

The world doesn't need another coaching platform. It needs you digitised, productised, and ready to scale on your terms.

The real flex? Building a business so aligned with who you are, you would never sell it. That's the unsellable model.

WHY MOST EXPERT BUSINESSES BREAK

Most "expert-led" businesses fall apart for one of two reasons:

1. **Too much YOU, but no system** → Everything relies on your energy. You're the bottleneck. It's not a business, it's a grind with a nice website.

2. **Too much SYSTEM, but no YOU** → You "scaled," but the soul's gone. You sound like a corporate chatbot. No one knows what makes you different.

We're here to land in the sweet spot:

- YOU at the centre
- SYSTEM around you
- Offers orbiting that system
- A flywheel that keeps spinning

No fluff. No bullshit. No burnout. Just a lean, profitable expert business that lets you work when you want, how you want, with the people you love working with.

THE FOUR COMPONENTS OF AN UNSELLABLE BUSINESS

What separates a true "unsellable" expert business from the rest? Four critical components:

1. **Personal IP That Creates Distance:** Your intellectual property, the frameworks, methods, and perspectives that only you could create become the foundation. This isn't generic knowledge; it's your specific lens for solving problems.

2. **Structured Delivery Systems:** You need ways to deliver your expertise that don't require your constant presence. This isn't about removing you; it's about extending you.

3. **Value-Based Pricing Architecture:** When you're the business, you don't compete on price. You create pricing tiers based on access, outcomes, and application, not hours worked.

4. **Self-Reinforcing Ecosystem:** Each element of your business feeds the others. A speech leads to a workshop. A workshop leads to a program. A program generates case studies. Those case studies lead to more speeches.

For a deeper exploration of how to structure these components into a complete business ecosystem, see Chapter 4 on the Expert Ecosystem Flywheel.

IMPLEMENTATION STEPS

ONE BIG THING:

Write a one-page brand statement that clearly articulates what makes your expertise unique and non-commoditisable.

Two Small Steps:

- Review your LinkedIn profile and remove any generic language that doesn't reflect your true voice
- List three ways your competitors describe themselves, then write alternatives that only you could claim

🎧 BEYOND THE PAGE

Scan for Steve's unfiltered insights and implementation hacks in this chapter. (2-3 min)

Not the audiobook. Better.

CHAPTER 2:

THE SELF-SPONSORED EXPERT MOVEMENT

Building Independence & Impact

"Waiting for someone to fund your genius? The only sponsorship worth having is the one where you back yourself first."

THE ESSENTIALS

- Being self-sponsored means betting on yourself—no investors, no plan B
- You're part of a new wave of experts: purpose-driven, self-sponsored, system-ready
- Your business should support your life, not consume it
- The 1:MANY:1 strategy is your secret weapon for selling to businesses
- Self-sponsorship gives you resilience, authenticity, and decisive leadership

CASE STUDY: JAMES & MIA — THE POWER OF SELF-SPONSORSHIP

BEFORE: James had 15 years of credibility but was struggling solo. Mia was fully booked but burning out from selling hours.

ACTION: James rejected investor offers and self-sponsored his business, building one workshop, one contact, and one $15,000 deal at a time. Mia shifted from selling hours to building a wellness movement with licensed programs.

AFTER:

- James retained 100% ownership and built true creative freedom
- Mia tripled her revenue while reducing delivery hours by 60%

"The moment I stopped looking for someone else to believe in me and started backing myself, everything changed."
— James

"I thought I had to choose between impact and freedom. I didn't." — Mia

NO PLAN B: THE SELF-SPONSORED PHILOSOPHY

Self-sponsored means no grants, no safety nets, no "just in case." It means building something because you have to, not because it looks good on LinkedIn.

It's grit over glamour. Substance over spin.

You don't wait for permission. You don't rely on hype. You back yourself with action.

You build a business that can scale on your terms, one that wraps around your lifestyle, not one that swallows it whole.

THE SELF-RELIANCE ADVANTAGE

The moment you stop waiting for external validation is the moment you become unstoppable.

While others chase funding, followers, and fame, the self-sponsored expert quietly builds systems that work, whether anyone's watching or not.

This approach gives you three critical advantages:

1. **Unmatched Resilience:** When your business isn't dependent on outside funding or fleeting trends, it can weather any storm.**Authentic Connection:** When you're not trying to be everything to everyone, you create deeper connections with the right people.**Rapid Decision-Making:** Without investors, boards, or trend-chasing to slow you down, you can pivot, adapt, and execute at speeds that make traditional businesses look like they're moving in slow motion.

THE UNSELLABLE BUSINESS: BUILT AROUND YOU BUT NOT DEPENDENT ON YOU

Let's get clear on what makes a business "unsellable":

It's a business you would never want to sell because it:

- Pays you incredibly well
- Aligns with your values and energy
- Is flexible enough to scale and rest
- Is so deeply "you" that no one else could do it justice

And while it's built around you, it's not dependent on you. That's the paradox.

THE STRUCTURAL PARADOX RESOLVED

Here's how the unsellable model resolves the apparent contradiction:

Your Expertise is the Core, Not the Limitation Your knowledge, perspective, and IP form the heart of the business, but your systems determine its reach. Your reputation opens doors, but your products and frameworks can travel without you.

In practice, this means you build systems, create products, and license your IP. You're never trapped in endless service delivery.

THE TRADITIONAL VS. SELF-SPONSORED APPROACH

Traditional Approach	Self-Sponsored Approach
Seek funding first, validate later	Validate with real clients, fund through revenue
Build audience, monetise eventually	Monetise first, scale audience strategically
Scale through hiring	Scale through systems and IP
Create based on market trends	Create based on lived experience
Success = exit strategy	Success = sustainable impact + profit

THE MOVEMENT YOU'RE BUILDING

You're not the only one sick of the hype and hustle.

The expert economy has been hijacked by marketing bros with fake urgency, coaches selling coaching to coaches, and endless funnels that lead nowhere.

But here's the shift: Experts are waking up. Companies are tired of canned content. The market is starving for substance.

And the edge now belongs to people like you, people with lived experience, a real point of view, who've done the work and are ready to be seen.

Welcome to the unsellable movement.

THE 1:MANY:1 STRATEGY: YOUR SECRET WEAPON

Here's the twist most experts miss:

You're not selling to individuals. You're selling to managers of employees who have a problem only your expertise can solve.

That's the "1:MANY:1" strategy:

- One conversation with the right manager
- Access to many employees
- Delivery that makes you repeatable, referable, and required

While everyone else is hawking $47 PDFs to burnt-out solopreneurs, you're:

- Licensing eLearns for $30k+
- Running team workshops for $10k+
- Offering hybrid programs with 95% margin
- Closing long-term partnerships instead of one-off transactions

You don't need a giant audience. You need a few of the right people to say yes.

To understand exactly which problems are most valuable in corporate settings, refer to Chapter 3, where we explore the specific criteria that make your expertise corporate-compatible.

THE UNSELLABLE MODEL IN ACTION

CASE STUDY: JAY'S IP LICENSING REVOLUTION

BEFORE: Jay had expertise in Cx and was running incredible high touch programs and consulting services, but had very little left over after receiving the invoice. Plus smaller customers couldn't afford the high ticket services.

THE TRANSFORMATION: We helped Jay transform her book into 25 self-directed eLearning modules.

THE RESULT: She now licenses her digital curriculum to companies for $20k–$50k per organisation, generating significant profit with minimal maintenance. Plus she is able to package the high margin eLearn's with live workshops for the ultimate high margin hybrid experience.

Case Study: Joey's Pre-Funded Development

BEFORE: Joey had a successful workshop program with high demand but low margins.

THE TRANSFORMATION: We created a digital mock-up and pre-sold it to an existing client for $20k before building.

THE RESULT: Once created, Joey could license that same program to other clients with nearly 100% margin - a digital asset generating revenue without constant delivery.

From Self-Sponsored to Self-Sustainable

Being self-sponsored doesn't mean doing everything yourself forever. It means building on your terms, with your values at the centre.

As your business grows, you'll still:

- Bring in team members who amplify your vision
- Create systems that give you breathing room

- Build assets that work while you don't

The difference is that these decisions come from a place of intention, not desperation.

You're not hiring because you're burnt out. You're not creating products because some guru told you to. You're building deliberately, with clear eyes and a steady hand.

YOUR PATH FORWARD

You've made it through the manifesto phase.

You've looked in the mirror. You've acknowledged that you're not just "in business"- you are the business. You've declared yourself a self-sponsored expert.

Now, you build the system.

The next part of this book is pure architecture, the Expert Ecosystem Flywheel that runs because of your expertise, not your exhaustion.

IMPLEMENTATION STEPS

ONE BIG THING:

Calculate your minimum viable revenue: the exact monthly amount you need to be sustainably self-sponsored.

Two Small Steps:

- Identify one corporate problem your expertise solves that has measurable cost implications
- List two revenue sources you could develop without external funding or permission

🎧 BEYOND THE PAGE

Scan for Steve's unfiltered insights and implementation hacks in this chapter. (2-3 min)

Not the audiobook. Better.

CHAPTER 3:

THE 3 MUST-HAVES TO BE IN THE CLUB

Who This Type of Business Is For

"No expertise, no money, no corporate problem? Then you're just a hobbyist with a LinkedIn profile. Harsh but true."

THE ESSENTIALS

- You must have expertise that solves a specific problem
- You must already be getting paid for your knowledge
- Your expertise must solve a problem that matters in corporate settings
- If you don't meet these criteria, focus on developing them first
- If you do meet them, you have everything needed to build an unsellable business

CASE STUDY: MICHAEL — THE HARD TRUTH THAT SAVED HIS BUSINESS

BEFORE: Three failed launches, $30k spent on marketing courses, no traction. Michael had expertise but no market recognition.

ACTION: We repositioned him around corporate burnout prevention, focusing on specific, urgent business problems.

AFTER:

- Secured his first corporate pilot program
- Built a growing, profitable client base

"I was creating solutions for problems nobody was paying to solve."

Look, this isn't a book for beginners.

It's not a "how to become an expert" book.

It's a "you're already an expert, now let's turn that into an empire you never want to sell" book.

And that means we have rules.

Three of them, in fact.

Three filters. Three gates. Three brutal lines in the sand.

Because this book is for people who are ready to build. Not dream. Not dabble. Do.

THE QUALIFICATION TRIFECTA

Before we dive into the architecture of the Unsellable ecosystem, you need to know if you're in the right place. This isn't about gatekeeping; it's about focusing your attention on where it matters.

Let's get clear on the three non-negotiable requirements that make the unsellable model work for you:

MUST-HAVE #1: YOU ARE AN EXPERT

You don't need to be the GOAT.

You just need to be a goat, as in, good at your shit.

Let's define "expert" the way real people do:

- You've helped people solve a specific problem
- You've been paid to do it
- You have a body of knowledge that's useful and repeatable
- You're a few chapters ahead of the people you serve

We're not talking about 10,000 hours.

We're talking about enough proof that someone has already trusted you to get results.

WHAT "EXPERT" REALLY MEANS

Being an expert doesn't mean you know everything. It means you know something valuable that others don't, and you can articulate it in a way that creates results.

You're an expert if:

- You have methodologies that you've developed through experience
- You can break down complex processes into teachable steps
- You've seen patterns that others haven't recognised yet
- You can predictably solve problems in your domain

If you're getting paid to think, speak, coach, consult, train, design, write, mentor, or teach, you're in.

If you've got frameworks in your head that others find valuable, you're in.

But if you're just starting out? Cool.

This book will still blow your mind.

But don't expect it to hold your hand. It's not that kind of book.

MUST-HAVE #2: YOU'RE ALREADY GETTING PAID

This isn't a "build your first course" handbook.

This is commercialisation for experts who are already being paid but are undervaluing their capacity.

So here's the rule:

You must already be earning money from your knowledge.

That can mean:

- You're a consultant on retainer
- You're doing keynote gigs

- You're running in-house workshops
- You're coaching clients
- You're delivering programs on behalf of someone else

You're in the game.

You've got clients, even if they're internal (as in, you're on salary but function like a specialist).

You're not trying to prove you're good. You're trying to scale how your goodness gets delivered.

THE REVENUE REALITY CHECK

Here's why this matters: The unsellable model isn't about creating initial market validation. It's about scaling what's already working.

Experts who try to skip this step often build products no one wants. They create elaborate systems with zero demand. They spend months developing offerings that solve problems no one is willing to pay for.

If you've already got revenue, even modest revenue, you've cleared the most important hurdle. You've proven someone values your expertise enough to exchange money for it.

Now, we can focus on leverage, not legitimacy.

MUST-HAVE #3: YOUR EXPERTISE SOLVES A PROBLEM THAT CORPORATE EMPLOYEES ACTUALLY HAVE

This is the clincher.

We're not here for life coaching for divorcees in Bali or TikTok hacks for teenagers with ADHD.

This book is built on a B2B model, solving real-world problems inside real companies with real employees who need to do their jobs better, faster, happier, or more effectively.

If your expertise:

- Makes teams more productive
- Helps leaders lead better
- Improves communication, mindset, operations, capability, wellbeing, retention, systems, customer experience...

Then guess what? You're in.

But here's the key difference:

You're not selling to the employee. You're selling to the manager of the employee.

That's the one-to-many-to-one model we live and die by in Unsellable.

One conversation. Many licenses. One client.

High scale, low friction. High margin, low bullshit.

CORPORATE-COMPATIBLE EXPERTISE

What makes expertise "corporate-compatible"? It solves problems that companies recognise, value, and budget for:

Problem Category	Examples
Performance	Productivity improvement, sales effectiveness, leadership development
Culture	Team collaboration, conflict resolution, diversity & inclusion
Systems	Process optimisation, change management, customer experience
Wellbeing	Stress management, burnout prevention, work-life integration

The key is that these problems are recognised by decision-makers who control budgets. They understand the cost of these problems and the value of solving them.

"What If I Don't Meet All Three?"

Then this book might hurt.

It'll frustrate you.

Because I'm going to move fast. I'm going to assume you have leverage points. I'm going to expect you to sell before you build. And I'm going to show you how to pitch to managers who actually control budgets.

If you don't meet the three must-haves yet? That's fine.

Your mission, then, is simple:

Get paid for your expertise in solving a company-relevant problem.

That's your only job right now.

The rest of this book will be here waiting when you're ready to plug it all in.

YOUR NEXT STEPS IF YOU'RE NOT READY

If you're not yet meeting all three criteria, here's your roadmap:

1. **If you're not yet an expert:** Focus on developing expertise in a specific problem area. Document your process, create a framework, and start helping people, even for free, to build your methodology.

2. **If you're not yet getting paid:** Package your expertise into a clear offering. Find someone with the problem you solve, and offer a solution at a price point that makes it easy to say yes.

3. **If your expertise isn't corporate-compatible:** Reframe your expertise through the lens of workplace impact. How does your knowledge improve performance, culture, systems, or well-being in a work context? This isn't about changing who you are. It's about positioning what you know in a way that opens doors to larger opportunities.

IF YOU MEET ALL THREE?

Congratulations.

You're in the club.

And not just in it. You're the one this book was written for.

From here on in, we're not starting from scratch.

We're starting from momentum.

And we're going to build on it.

THE OPPORTUNITY AHEAD

What happens when you combine true expertise, proven demand, and corporate compatibility?

You get the foundation for a business that can:

- Generate $500K+ in annual revenue with minimal overhead
- Create predictable cash flow without constant marketing
- Build assets that appreciate in value while reducing your workload
- Position you as the category leader in your niche
- Give you the freedom to work when, where, and how you want

This isn't hyperbole. It's what happens when you apply the unsellable model to expertise that meets all three criteria.

Once you've confirmed you meet these three criteria, head to Chapter 4 to discover how to structure your expertise into the Expert Ecosystem Flywheel, the engine that will power your unsellable business.

IMPLEMENTATION STEPS

ONE BIG THING:

Honestly assess which of the three must-haves you currently meet and create a 30-day plan to address any gaps.

Two Small Steps:

- Document evidence of your expertise (gather testimonials, results, case studies)
- Identify one corporate department that would benefit most from your expertise

🎧 BEYOND THE PAGE

Scan for Steve's unfiltered insights and implementation hacks in this chapter. (2-3 min)

Not the audiobook. Better.

PART

II

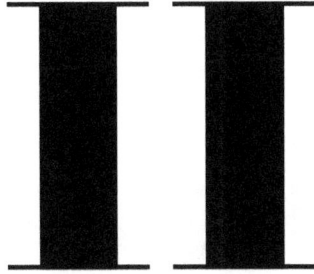

THE ECOSYSTEM

"Systems amplify genius. A framework outlasts inspiration. When your knowledge transforms into an ecosystem, it creates a value machine that works even when you don't."

CHAPTER 4:

THE EXPERT ECOSYSTEM FLYWHEEL

The Parts Without the Machine

"One workshop makes you money. A whole ecosystem makes you wealthy. Stop selling moments and start building momentum."

THE ESSENTIALS

- The Flywheel has 7 cogs: Book, eLearn, Hybrid Program, Workshop, Keynote, Coaching, Consulting
- The workshop is often the hidden catalyst that unlocks your entire ecosystem
- Each cog monetises your IP in a different way with different scale/value combinations
- Don't build them all at once, build strategically based on what you already have
- The more cogs you connect, the faster your ecosystem grows

CASE STUDY: ELENA - FROM ONE-OFF WINS TO PERPETUAL MOTION

BEFORE: Elena delivered brilliant ops results but had to hustle for every new client. No retention. No momentum.

ACTION: We built her Expert Ecosystem Flywheel: book → eLearn → Hybrid → Workshop → Keynote → Consulting

AFTER:

- Increased client lifetime value by 340%
- Created continuous revenue without constant prospecting

"I used to deliver isolated wins. Now I create unstoppable momentum."

Let me guess.

You've got a book. Or a keynote. Or a workshop. Or a coaching program. Or a framework you draw on napkins that people love.

But here's the problem:

You've got parts of the machine... but the machine's not running.

You're pushing instead of spinning. You're surviving instead of scaling. You're booked and broke.

That's not a business. That's burnout in slow motion.

Enter: the Expert Ecosystem Flywheel.

THE MISSING STRUCTURE

Most experts struggle not from a lack of value but from a lack of structure.

You've created a brilliant IP. You've delivered it successfully. You've been paid for your thinking.

But it's all isolated. Disconnected. Episodic.

You finish one gig, and it's back to the hunt. You deliver one workshop, and it's a one-off victory.

The solution isn't working harder. It's working differently.

WHAT IS THE FLYWHEEL?

It's the model that lets your ideas:

- Get seen
- Get bought
- Get delivered
- Get repeated
- Get referred

Without you having to start from scratch every time.

It's a circular, self-sustaining, lean ecosystem that wraps around your existing IP and amplifies your ability to monetise it without exhausting yourself.

You stop trading time. You start leveraging output. And the more you use it, the faster it spins.

The Physics of Expert Business Growth

Traditional business growth is linear:

1. Create something
2. Sell it
3. Deliver it
4. Repeat

Flywheel growth is exponential:

1. Create something once
2. Package it multiple ways
3. Let each package feed the others
4. Watch momentum build

Think of it like a heavy wheel that's difficult to start turning but, once in motion, requires minimal energy to maintain and accelerate.

THE 7 CORE COGS OF THE EXPERT ECOSYSTEM

These aren't "ideas." These are products.

Each one monetises your thinking in a different way. Each one has a different relationship between revenue and scale.

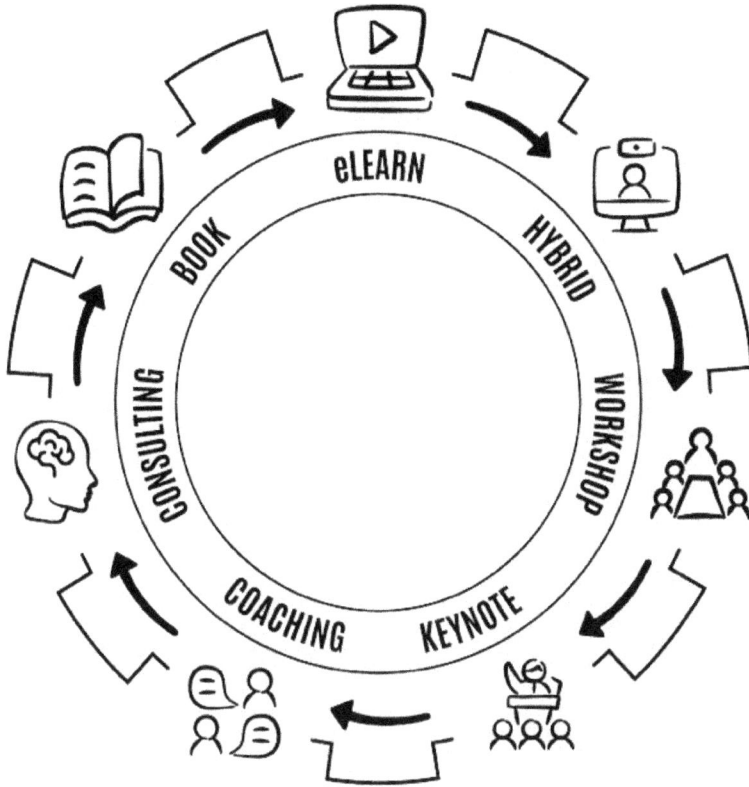

Let's break them down:

1. The Book

- Low cost, high scale
- Establishes authority
- Sits at the top of funnel
- Can be licensed in bulk to companies
- Becomes the launchpad for every other cog

2. The Self-Directed eLearn

- The anchor
- Off-the-shelf → Branded → Custom

- Infinite scale, 95% margin
- Delivers your content 24/7, company-wide
- Can be hosted on your LMS or theirs

3. The Hybrid Program

- Self-directed + live touchpoints
- Best of both worlds
- Lower time from you, higher perceived value for them
- Great for multi-year contracts

4. The Workshop

- Live training, face-to-face or virtual
- High-impact, high-energy, limited scale
- Easily productised and replicated
- Great way to beta-test ideas before you build them
- The hidden catalyst that can unlock multiple other cogs

5. The Keynote

- Gateway drug
- Low time, high exposure
- Not the goal, but a strategic piece of the puzzle
- Can lead to licensing, workshops, and eLearn deals

6. The Coaching Offer

- High touch, high trust
- Great for individuals, exec teams, or SMEs
- Limited scale, use strategically
- Often a bolt-on or premium layer

7. The Consulting / Advisory Offer

- Your highest-dollar item
- You're paid to think and solve
- Should never be discounted
- Use this to fund the build of the rest of your ecosystem

THE WORKSHOP: YOUR ECOSYSTEM CATALYST

While every cog has its purpose, the workshop requires special attention. It is the most accessible entry point for most experts, and it is the quickest way to gain access to a variety of additional ecosystem components.

Why? Because almost any expert can design and deliver a workshop immediately, with minimal preparation time or technical complexity. If someone asked you to run a session tomorrow and offered you $2-5k, you could do it. Of course, you can.

But the real magic happens after that workshop:

- Record it: Instantly have raw material for an eLearn
- Break it into modules: Framework for a hybrid program
- Extract key frameworks: Content for your book
- Collect testimonials: Proof for your marketing

One well-executed workshop can spawn 3-4 other cogs with minimal additional work. It's the perfect starting point for your ecosystem, regardless of where you are now.

For specific strategies on how to choose and build your next cog, see Chapter 5, in which we explore the "Next Door Neighbour" method and pre-selling techniques.

COG POSITIONING: THE VALUE VS. SCALE MATRIX

Understanding where each cog sits in terms of value delivery and scalability is critical for strategic planning:

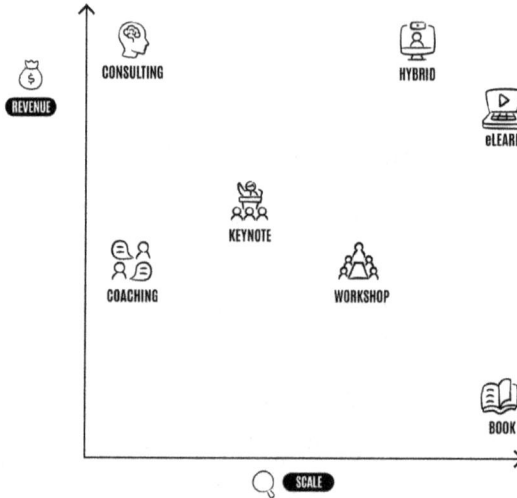

Cog	Revenue potential	Scalability	Best Use
Book	Low	Unlimited	Lead generation, authority building
eLearn	Medium–High	Unlimited	Recurring revenue, corporate deployment
Hybrid	High	Medium	Blending impact with efficiency
Workshop	Med/High	Low/Med	Relationship building, idea testing
Keynote	Med/High	Medium	Visibility, opening doors
Coaching	Med	Very Low	Premium offering, deep impact
Consulting	High	Very Low	Highest revenue, strategic funding

This matrix helps you determine which cogs to develop first based on your current needs and resources.

HERE'S THE MAGIC: THE COGS DON'T WORK IN ISOLATION- THEY COMPOUND

One keynote can lead to five workshop bookings. One workshop can lead to a request for an eLearn version. One eLearn can lead to a hybrid rollout. One hybrid can lead to a $100k+ consulting retainer.

The flywheel works because you've built the options. It spins because you're not starting from scratch every time.

THE PATH OF A CLIENT THROUGH YOUR ECOSYSTEM

Let's map an actual client journey through the ecosystem:

1. **Entry Point:** HR Director attends your keynote at an industry conference

2. **First Purchase:** Books you for a leadership workshop for their management team

3. **Expansion:** Requests a digital version (eLearn) to roll out company-wide

4. **Deepening:** Adds coaching for key executives as a premium layer

5. **Strategic Partnership:** Retains you as an advisor to develop a custom implementation

Each step increases:

- Revenue per client
- Relationship depth
- Implementation success
- Referral potential

And all without you having to find new clients for each transaction.

THE COGS ARE MODULAR, BUT BUILT TO CONNECT

You don't need all 7 to start.

But the more you build, the faster it moves, and the harder it is for competitors to touch you.

Each cog can lead to the next.

This isn't a ladder. It's a circular engine.

And when the flywheel is running, here's what happens:

- You build once, sell forever
- You never have to discount
- You have multiple entry points for clients
- You can scale without cloning yourself
- You can respond to any budget or timeline without lowering your standards

STARTING WHERE YOU ARE: MAPPING YOUR CURRENT ASSETS

Before you rush to build what's missing, inventory what you already have:

1. **Content Assessment:** What IP have you already created? (books, slides, frameworks, methods)
2. **Delivery Assessment:** What formats have you already mastered? (speaking, training, coaching)
3. **Client Assessment:** What have clients already requested but you couldn't deliver?
4. **Gap Assessment:** Which cogs would create the most immediate impact?

The goal isn't to build the entire flywheel at once. It's to identify your strongest starting point and build from there.

THE SECRET = PRODUCTISING YOU

None of this works if you don't understand the core idea:

You are not a deliverable. You are a system.

Each cog is a different way of delivering that system.

The book = the pitch. The eLearn = the product. The keynote = the bait. The workshop = the bridge. The coaching = the insight. The consulting = the premium solution.

Together? You're unstoppable.

IMPLEMENTATION PRIORITY FRAMEWORK

How do you decide which cogs to build first? Follow this framework:

1. Start with what you have: Which cogs are already built or nearly built?

2. Follow client demand: What are clients already asking for?

3. Balance quick wins with long-term assets: Aim for one immediate revenue generator and one scalable asset

4. Build your funding machine first: Use high-dollar, high-value cogs to fund the development of scale-oriented cogs

For most experts, starting with a workshop is the fastest path to building multiple cogs. It generates immediate revenue while creating the raw material for more scalable assets.

IMPLEMENTATION STEPS

ONE BIG THING:

Take the Expert Readiness Diagnostic to identify which cogs you should prioritise building next.

Two Small Steps:

- Map your current offerings on the Value vs. Scale Matrix
- Design the outline for a 90-minute workshop based on your core expertise (even without a client)

🎧 BEYOND THE PAGE

Scan for Steve's unfiltered insights and implementation hacks in this chapter. (2-3 min)

Not the audiobook. Better.

CHAPTER 5:

STRATEGIC BUILDING: CHOOSE, PRE-SELL, THEN BUILD

The Strategy for Growth Without Risk

"The best next step isn't across town. It's right next door to what's already working. And never build it before someone pays for it."

THE ESSENTIALS

- Choose the cog that's closest to what's already working for you
- The workshop is the hidden catalyst that unlocks your entire ecosystem
- Use the "Next Door Neighbour" method to maximise existing content
- Never build before someone says yes to buying it
- Use mock-ups to validate your idea and generate early sales
- Let your clients bankroll the build with deposits and pre-payments

CASE STUDY: RYAN & SOPHIE — THE PRE-SELL SUCCESS STORIES

BEFORE: Ryan made $180k/year running 20 sales workshops and hit a ceiling. Sophie was planning to spend a year building a flagship course without market validation.

ACTION: Ryan recorded one workshop and turned it into an eLearn. Sophie created a one-page mockup and pitched it before building anything.

AFTER:

- Ryan doubled his revenue in six months while cutting delivery days by 25%
- Sophie generated $30,000 in pre-sales before building anything

"I already had everything I needed. I just hadn't captured it to scale." — Ryan

"If I hadn't tested first, I would've built something no one wanted." — Sophie

So you've seen the flywheel. You're ready to go full beast mode and build all seven cogs at once.

But hold up, cowboy.

You don't need everything. You just need the next thing, the next cog that gives you the biggest bang for the least effort, based on what you've already got.

And once you choose it, you're going to sell it before you build it.

The whole point of Unsellable is to de-risk your business— we're not here to hustle. We're here to build leverage with minimal risk.

PART 1: CHOOSE THE RIGHT COG FIRST

THE WORKSHOP: YOUR ECOSYSTEM CATALYST

Let's talk about the one cog that unlocks everything else: the workshop.

Here's why the workshop is so powerful:

- **Immediate Revenue:** Unlike a book or digital program, you can create and deliver a workshop tomorrow if a client asks.

- **Low Development Cost:** You already have the expertise in your head. A simple slide deck and some interactive exercises are all you need to get started.

- **The Domino Effect:** One workshop creates a cascade of other cogs:

- Record the workshop → Raw footage for your eLearn

- Break it into modules → Framework for your hybrid program

- Package the slides → First draft of your book content

- Get testimonials → Proof for your marketing

If you only build one new cog, make it a workshop. Then, use that workshop to unlock everything else.

The "Next Door Neighbour" Method

Your next product shouldn't be 12 suburbs away from what you already do. It should be right next door—the closest, simplest, most logical extension of what's already working.

Here's how this works:

- **Got a book?** Next cog = Workshop → eLearn → Hybrid

- **Got a workshop?** Next cog = eLearn → Book → Hybrid

- **Got a keynote?** Next cog = Workshop → eLearn

- **Got a coaching offer?** Next cog = Group workshop → Self-directed program

- **Got consulting gigs?** Next cog = Workshop → eLearn → Book

CHOOSE YOUR COG CHEAT SHEET

What You Have	Next Best Cog(s)
Book	Workshop → eLearn → Hybrid
Workshop	eLearn → Hybrid
Keynote	Workshop → eLearn
Coaching	Group → Digital → Templates
Consulting	Workshop → eLearn → Hybrid
Course (old/broken)	Modernise → eLearn → Hybrid

The question to ask is simple: **What's Already Working That I Can Package Better?**

Look at your current engagements:

- What's getting the best feedback?
- What are you repeating again and again?
- What do you wish you could automate?
- What do clients always ask for next?

The answer is your next cog.

PART 2: PRE-SELL IT BEFORE YOU BUILD IT

Now that you've chosen your next cog, here's the rule that will save you months of wasted effort: **You Sell It First, THEN You Build It.**

THE CREATE-FIRST FALLACY

Most "experts" are broke because they build first and sell later. They spend months polishing a course, over-engineering a framework, and designing modules they think people want, only to launch to crickets.

It's not because your content isn't good. It's because you built something before anyone said yes.

THE PRE-SELL METHOD

Here's how to sell before you build:

1. **Create a simple mock-up:** A lightweight preview of what your program could look like, not the full course, just the teaser. Include a one-pager on what it solves, a rough outline, a few visuals, and pricing options. **Position it as "in development":** Create exclusivity and room for input.

2. **Offer early partner pricing:** Discount in exchange for feedback.

3. **Set clear timelines:** When they'll get what you're creating.

4. **Use the deposit to fund creation:** Their money builds your asset.

The ideal mock-up should be:

- Visually appealing: Shows potential
- Substantive enough: Demonstrates expertise
- Clearly unfinished: Leaves room for input
- Outcome-focused: Emphasises results
- Confidently priced: Shows value

This pre-sell approach aligns perfectly with the pricing strategy outlined in Chapter 9, where you'll learn how to articulate value-based pricing that makes these pre-sales even more effective.

THE MAGIC ONE-SENTENCE EMAIL

Here's the email that's generated hundreds of thousands in pre-sales:

"Hey [Client], we're thinking of offering [insert next cog based on what they've already experienced with you]. Would you be interested in being one of the first to try it?"

That's it. After you've delivered a workshop, this simple email can unlock funding for your eLearn. After they've licensed your eLearn, this email can create a hybrid program opportunity.

THE BUILD RULES (WRITE THESE ON YOUR DAMN WALL)

1. Never build from scratch. Always start with what's already proven.

2. Never build before you sell. Use a mock-up, pitch it, and build once someone commits.

3. Never build too far from home. Stay close to your genius. One step at a time.

4. Never build alone. You've got us. Learn Awesome. The movement. The playbook.

PRO TIP: CLIENTS PREFER THIS

You think clients want polish. But what they really want is partnership.

Founding clients love:

- Being first
- Getting influence in the design
- Beta pricing
- Feeling part of something

- Knowing they're not buying something off the shelf

This isn't just de-risking it for you, it's creating buy-in for them.

THE ONE-WORKSHOP ROADMAP

Here's exactly how one workshop becomes a complete ecosystem:

1. Develop a 90-minute workshop on your core expertise
2. Book it with one client using the one-sentence email
3. Record the delivery (with proper permissions)
4. Create a mock-up of an eLearn using screenshots from the recording
5. Email existing clients: "After running this workshop for [Company X], we're developing a digital version. Would you like to be one of our first licensing partners?"
6. Use the licensing payment to properly produce the eLearn
7. Bundle the eLearn with quarterly live sessions to create your hybrid program
8. Extract key content for a book or lead magnet

IMPLEMENTATION STEPS

ONE BIG THING:

Create a simple one-page mockup of your next cog based on what's already working.

Two Small Steps:

- Draft the one-sentence email to 5 potential clients about your new offering

- List what materials you already have that could be repurposed for this new cog

🎧 BEYOND THE PAGE

Scan for Steve's unfiltered insights and implementation hacks in this chapter. (2-3 min)

Not the audiobook. Better.

CHAPTER 6

YOUR TECH STACK CAN'T BE SHIT

The Tech Tangle

"Your tech stack is like plumbing. Nobody notices until it leaks all over the carpet. Then it's the only thing anyone can talk about."

THE ESSENTIALS

- You need one integrated system to run your business, not a dozen disconnected tools
- Your tech must handle CRM, calendar, communications, sales, and delivery
- Client experience is directly impacted by how smooth your systems run
- Keep it lean and functional, fancy features don't matter if the basics don't work
- Budget time and resources to properly set up your tech foundation

CASE STUDY: ALEX — FROM TECH CHAOS TO STREAMLINED SUCCESS

BEFORE: Seven disconnected platforms. Constant admin headaches. Lost deals due to tech failures.

ACTION: We consolidated everything into one seamless system, from booking to billing.

AFTER:

- Cut admin time by 70%
- Increased proposal close rates by 30%
- Boosted client retention by 30%

> *"I thought tech was just a necessary evil.*
> *Done right, it became my secret weapon."*

If you're like most experts, you've got a tech stack that looks like your junk drawer:

- MailChimp from 2017

- A random PDF lead magnet that no longer works
- An outdated course on Teachable you forgot you even made
- Fifteen Google Sheets you're too scared to delete
- And a calendar link that somehow double-books itself every time

It's time to stop the madness.

You're not a tech guru. You're an expert.

You don't need more tools. You need the right system.

This chapter is not about becoming a nerd.

This is about protecting your time, preserving your energy, and setting up a backend that does the heavy lifting so you don't have to.

THE HIDDEN COST OF TECH CHAOS

Every minute you spend troubleshooting tech is a minute you're not:

- Delivering value
- Creating IP
- Closing deals
- Building relationships
- Doing the work you actually enjoy

Tech problems aren't just annoying. They're expensive. They drain your time, energy, and credibility.

THE PROBLEM WITH MOST EXPERT TECH STACKS

Too many moving parts. Too many platforms. Too many zaps and bandaids and "I'll fix that laters".

You've got:

- A CRM that doesn't talk to your email tool
- An LMS that looks like it's from 2004
- A booking system that ghosted your last client
- And a VA who's about to quit because nothing ever works

You're bleeding time. You're leaking credibility. You're losing deals because the backend is duct-taped to hell.

And here's the worst part: it doesn't need to be this way.

THE EXPERT TECH TRAP

Most experts fall into one of two tech traps:

The Minimalist Mess: You've avoided tech decisions entirely. You're running everything through Gmail, spreadsheets, and text messages. It works when you're small, but it's completely unscalable.

The Frankenstack: You've cobbled together a dozen different tools as you've grown. Each one solves a specific problem, but nothing works together. You're the human API trying to make it all connect.

Both approaches guarantee you'll hit a ceiling, either in revenue, sanity, or both.

THE RULE: ONE SYSTEM TO RUN THE SHOW

Here's what we believe:

You need one central brain. One operating system.

A single place that handles: Marketing, Sales, Delivery, Nurture, Admin and Scale.

At Learn Awesome, we run all our clients and experts through one absolute beast of a platform: GoHighLevel.

And here's why:

- One login
- One calendar
- One contact list
- One dashboard
- Emails, SMS, DMs, landing pages, contracts, pipelines, courses, all in ONE place
- And you own it. You control it. You drive it.

No more 18 tools to manage one business.

Just a central command centre that's scalable, affordable, and doesn't explode every time you sneeze.

THE INTEGRATED SYSTEM ADVANTAGE

When everything lives in one place:

- No more double data entry
- No more lost leads between systems
- No more "which platform was that client in again?"
- No more integration failures
- No more password resets for 12 different tools

You get a single view of your entire business, from first touch to repeat client.

Your tech stack directly supports the marketing and sales funnels covered in Chapters 7 and 8. A solid tech foundation makes those funnels infinitely more effective.

WHAT YOUR SYSTEM MUST DO

Whether you use GoHighLevel (our ride-or-die) or something else, your system must be able to:

- Send emails + SMS + DMs
- Store your contacts + tag them properly
- Host your booking links + sync with your calendar
- Automate reminders + follow-ups
- Manage your sales pipeline (aka "who's ready to buy")
- Handle forms, surveys, and applications
- Send invoices + take payments
- Host or connect to your learning content
- Connect to your funnels
- Let you see it all in one dashboard

If your system can't do that?

You're not running a business. You're managing chaos.

THE CLIENT EXPERIENCE MATTERS

Your tech stack isn't just about your convenience, it's about how clients experience working with you:

Poor Tech Experience	Integrated System Experience
Multiple logins	Single portal access
Inconsistent branding	Cohesive brand experience
Manual follow-ups	Automated touchpoints

Lost information	Everything in one place
Delayed responses	Instant confirmations
Payment hassles	Seamless transactions

Remember: Your clients judge your expertise partly by how smoothly you operate. A janky backend makes everything you do seem less professional.

Keep It Lean. Build It Once. Make It Last.

The goal here is not complexity.

The goal is to:

- Simplify
- Streamline
- Systemise
- So you can spend more time creating, connecting, and cashing cheques.

Let tech do what tech does best, the repeatable, annoying shit.

Let you do what you do best: thinking, building, leading, creating, and selling.

The Essential Tech Checklist

Before you add any new tool to your stack, ask:

1. Does this replace multiple existing tools?
2. Does it integrate seamlessly with my core system?
3. Will it scale as my business grows?
4. Is it reliable enough for client-facing use?
5. Can I delegate the management of it?

If the answer to any of these is "no," think twice.

BONUS TIP: USE LEARN AWESOME'S SYSTEM

If you're part of the Expert Incubator, you already know:

We give our experts access to our full CRM and backend system. We set it up. We support it. We will show you how to run it.

Because we don't want your genius getting blocked by bullshit tech.

So yeah, you can stitch together 18 different tools, pay for 10 logins, and pray your Zapier flows don't break every other week...

OR

You can plug into our all-in-one and just get to work.

Tech Implementation Timeline

If you're ready to consolidate your tech stack, here's a realistic timeline:

Week	Focus Area	Key Actions
1-2	Assessment	Inventory current tools and identify gaps
3-4	Selection	Choose your core platform (we recommend GoHighLevel)
5-6	Migration	Move contacts and content to new system
7-8	Automation	Set up workflows and templates
9-10	Testing	Ensure everything works as expected
11-12	Optimisation	Refine and improve based on actual use

This isn't an overnight process, but it's an investment that pays dividends for years.

The LMS Question

"But what about an LMS? Don't I need some fancy learning platform to deliver my content?"

Look, I hear this question constantly. And here's the truth:

Most experts waste massive amounts of time and money building learning platforms they don't need yet. They're putting the cart ten miles ahead of the horse.

Here's the B2B reality: When you're selling to companies, they often want your content on THEIR system, not yours. They've already invested in their corporate LMS, and they want everything centralized there. Or they'll want a white-labeled solution they can call their own.

So what should you do?

Step 1: Use the tech stack we've outlined for everything else (marketing, sales, delivery, admin)

Step 2: Focus on creating great content, not building infrastructure

Step 3: When a client specifically requests to host content on your platform, use the "sell before you build" approach:

- Create a mockup of "your academy"
- Price it properly (remember, they're paying for the solution, not the tech)
- Use their payment to fund the actual build

This is how we do it for all the experts we work with at Learn Awesome.

"The first project of a new thing will always be a reactive build."

You either bake the time to build it into your pricing, or you get a team like Learn Awesome to build it for you.

Better still, for our experts, we even rent you some space on the

Learn Awesome LMS, so no matter what, you have something world-class to offer while your own academy is being built. (No pressure, just saying. We're helpful like that.)

Let's talk economics for a second. Setting up your own academy for the B2C market might get you one $500 sale at a time. Meanwhile, that same self-directed eLearn sold to a company with 300 employees could bring in $15k+ in one deal. Which approach do you think better funds your academy investment?

The B2B approach means your clients literally pay for your infrastructure development, providing both the commitment and investment you need to build properly.

Too many experts have this backward. They invest in online academy infrastructure, hoping for individual clients when they should be focussing on developing corporate relationships and infrastructure.

The rule is simple: Don't build tech until you have paying clients who need it. Your academy can come later, funded by the very people who'll use it.

IMPLEMENTATION STEPS

ONE BIG THING:

Audit your current tech stack and create a 90-day consolidation plan with specific milestones.

Two Small Steps:

- List the 3 biggest tech-related frustrations in your current business
- Schedule 2 hours this week dedicated solely to tech improvements

🎧 BEYOND THE PAGE

Scan for Steve's unfiltered insights and implementation hacks in this chapter. (2-3 min)

Not the audiobook. Better.

III

ACQUISITION & SALES

"The art of acquisition isn't convincing everyone you're valuable. It's ensuring the right people can find you when they need you most. True sales is the courage to price transformation, not time."

CHAPTER 7

MARKETING THAT DOESN'T MAKE YOU HATE YOURSELF

The Content Creation Trap

"If your marketing plan involves dancing on social media, we need to have a chat. Talk directly to people who can pay you. The rest is just noise."

THE ESSENTIALS

- You only need two types of marketing: Outreach and Content

- Focus on where decision-makers look, not where everyone else is posting

- Outreach gets clients now, Content builds your pipeline for later

- Make every piece of content lead somewhere specific (to a call, download, etc.)

- Be findable and undeniable where it matters, not omnipresent everywhere

CASE STUDY: LENA - THE FOCUSED STRATEGY THAT OUTPERFORMED CONSTANT CONTENT

BEFORE: Daily posting. Weekly newsletters. Zero quality leads. Total burnout.

ACTION: We scrapped the "be everywhere" model, focusing solely on LinkedIn and direct outreach to decision-makers.

AFTER:

- Tripled her lead quality in 90 days

- Reduced marketing time by 60%

> *"It's not about being everywhere. It's about being findable and undeniable to the right people."*

Let's be honest.

Most marketing advice for experts is:

- Shallow

- Soul-destroying
- And built for broke coaches who think content = credibility

You've seen it all: "Post 3x per day!" "Just deliver value!" "Go viral!" "Document your journey!" "Be authentic!" (aka be fake in a slightly different way)

And what does it get you?

- A few likes
- A few dopamine hits
- And still no sales

Here's the reality:

You don't need to go viral. You don't need 10k followers. You need to be visible and valuable to the right people.

That's it.

The Expert Marketing Dilemma

Most experts face a constant tension:

- Be everywhere or be invisible
- Dance for the algorithm or be forgotten
- Create content daily or lose momentum

It's exhausting. It's unsustainable. And worst of all, it rarely converts to actual business.

The problem isn't your commitment or creativity. It's that you're following a playbook designed for influencers, not experts with real IP to sell.

THE MARKETING STRATEGY THAT ACTUALLY WORKS FOR EXPERTS

Here's how we break it down in Unsellable:

You need just two types of marketing: Outreach and Content.

That's it.

One brings them in. The other builds trust while they circle the runway.

And both need to be built on one golden rule: "Be findable and undeniable."

Let's unpack that.

THE FINDABLE & UNDENIABLE FRAMEWORK

Element	What It Means	Why It Matters
Findable	You appear where decision-makers look	You can't help people who can't find you
Undeniable	Your expertise is clearly evident	Credibility eliminates competition

This framework replaces vanity metrics with visibility that actually matters to your business growth.

OUTREACH — GET IN THE ROOM

This is the fast lane.

The no-fluff, no-funnels, no-fkn-around strategy.

You find the people. You talk to the people. You make offers to the people.

Who?

- Managers of employees with the problem you solve
- L&D, HR, People & Culture leads
- Execs, team leads, business unit heads
- People with budget and urgency

How?

- LinkedIn DMs
- Email
- Introductions
- Referrals
- Conference lists
- Workshop attendees
- Past clients
- Your network (stop sleeping on it)

What Do You Say?

Keep it stupidly simple:

"Hey [Name], I've been helping [X type of company] with [Y problem] using [Z type of solution]. Would love to share what we're seeing, keen to chat?"

That's it. Start the convo. Get the meeting.

Then, let your expert ecosystem do the talking.

These outreach techniques set the stage for the sales conversations covered in Chapter 11, where you'll learn the PACER framework for converting interested prospects into clients.

OUTREACH THAT GETS RESPONSES

The difference between spam and strategic outreach is specificity:

Weak Outreach	Strong Outreach
"I help companies improve productivity"	"I've been helping tech companies reduce onboarding time by 40%"

"Would love to connect and explore synergies"	"Would love to share what we're seeing in the finance sector"
"Check out my lead magnet"	"I noticed your team is expanding, perfect timing for our retention framework"
"Let me know if you're interested"	"Would Tuesday at 2pm work for a quick call?"

The key is to sound like a peer with valuable insight, not a desperate vendor.

CONTENT — STAY TOP OF MIND

If outreach is how you hunt, content is how you plant seeds.

You don't need to be a content creator. You don't need to be a guru. You just need to show up consistently and show that you know your shit.

Authority isn't built through virality. It's built through relevance.

Post content that does one of four things:

- Shows you understand the problem
- Offers a perspective shift
- Teaches something useful
- Demonstrates results or stories

Where?

- LinkedIn (non-negotiable for B2B)
- Email (short, punchy, valuable)
- Podcast guest spots (borrowed credibility)
- Articles, blogs, whitepapers (optional)
- Conference talks (repurpose forever)

THE EXPERT CONTENT MATRIX

Content Type	Purpose	Frequency	Example
Insight Posts	Demonstrate expertise	1-2x/week	"The 3 hidden causes of team burnout most leaders miss"
Case Studies	Prove results	2-4x/month	"How we helped [Company] reduce turnover by 32%"
Frameworks	Show your methods	1-2x/month	"Our 4-part system for accelerating team integration"
Contrarian Takes	Stand out	1-2x/month	"Why traditional onboarding actually creates turnover"

The goal isn't volume. It's strategic impact on the right audience.

THE ONE PLATFORM RULE

Pick one. Dominate it. Don't spread yourself thin trying to be on every app with a login screen.

If you're in B2B, LinkedIn is your arena.

Not as a personal diary. Not as an engagement farm. As a platform to prove your value and stay visible to buyers.

PLATFORM SELECTION STRATEGY

For most B2B experts, the hierarchy is clear:

1.   LinkedIn - The non-negotiable base

2.   Email - Your owned audience

3. Podcast Guesting - Borrowed credibility

4. Speaking - High-leverage visibility

Everything else is optional. Better to do 1-2 channels well than 5-6 poorly.

THE YIN AND YANG OF OUTREACH + CONTENT

- Outreach = Fast. Targeted. Sales-focused.
- Content = Slow burn. Visibility. Trust-building.

You don't need to do both at the same intensity. But you do need to do both consistently.

Here's a simple rule:

If you don't want to post content? Double down on outreach. If you hate sales calls? Get really good at content. But if you want a serious business? Do both.

STRATEGIC TIME ALLOCATION

Marketing Type	Time Commitment	Expected ROI	Timeline
Outreach	5-7 hours/ week	High	1-4 weeks
Content	2-4 hours/ week	Medium-High	1-6 months

Outreach gets you clients now. Content builds your pipeline for later. Both are essential for sustainable growth.

PRO TIP: MAKE YOUR CONTENT LEAD SOMEWHERE

It's not enough to "educate your audience."

You need calls to action that point to your flywheel:

- "Grab the book"
- "Watch the video"
- "Book a call"
- "Join the list"
- "Get the self-assessment"
- "Join the beta"
- "See our eLearn in action"

No CTA? No point.

THE CONTENT-TO-CONVERSION PATH

Your content should create a clear path to your ecosystem:

1. Awareness Content → Demonstrates you understand the problem
2. Solution Content → Shows you have a unique approach
3. Proof Content → Establishes that your approach works
4. Opportunity Content → Creates openings to engage deeper

Each piece should move prospects one step closer to your ecosystem flywheel.

BONUS MOVE: MARKETING AS A TROJAN HORSE

The best marketing doesn't just build awareness, it sets the sale up in advance.

- Every post should show that you understand your market
- Every DM should sound like a peer, not a pitch
- Every workshop you run should end with, "Want to go deeper?"

- Every podcast you're on should point to a page that sells something

Don't create "content." Create momentum.

MARKETING WITHOUT EXHAUSTION

The sustainable approach:

- Batch content creation (monthly, not daily)
- Use templates for outreach (personalise key elements)
- Repurpose everything (one talk becomes 10 posts)
- Focus on conversion, not vanity metrics
- Measure what matters (meetings set, not likes received)

This is marketing that builds your business without burning you out.

IMPLEMENTATION STEPS

ONE BIG THING:

Choose one platform to dominate and create a content calendar with eight pieces of expertise-demonstrating content.

Two Small Steps:

- Identify 5 potential clients you could reach out to directly this week
- Create one clear call-to-action that all your content will point toward

🎧 BEYOND THE PAGE

Scan for Steve's unfiltered insights and implementation hacks in this chapter. (2-3 min)

Not the audiobook. Better.

CHAPTER 8:

THE TWO FUNNELS THAT FEED THE MACHINE

The Funnel Fallacy

"Your funnel doesn't need more bells and whistles. It needs to work. Two solid pathways beat a dozen half-baked ideas every time."

THE ESSENTIALS

- You only need two funnels: Book Funnel and VSL (Video Sales Letter) Funnel
- Book Funnel builds authority and your list, VSL Funnel generates qualified sales calls
- These funnels connect directly to your Expert Ecosystem
- Simplicity trumps complexity in funnel design, focus on what works
- Both funnels should be tied to your CRM for tracking and nurturing

CASE STUDY: MARCUS - TWO FUNNELS, 10X THE RESULTS

BEFORE: Marcus was buried under 12 half-finished funnels. High spend. Low return.

ACTION: We scrapped everything and built two funnels: a Book Funnel for authority and a VSL Funnel for qualification and sales.

AFTER:

- Lead costs dropped 50%
- Conversion rates doubled
- Marketing workload slashed

> *"Complexity doesn't equal sophistication. Simplicity scales faster."*

Here's a problem:

Most experts overthink their funnels like they're building the Death Star.

- 47-email nurture sequences
- 9-step webinar funnels
- Tripwires, exit pops, upsells, downsells, post-ups, backflips
- And they still end up with... no leads and no money

It's chaos disguised as strategy.

And it's time to end it.

At Learn Awesome, and across the entire Unsellable ecosystem, we run two funnels (maybe three if we're lucky.)

And they work.

THE MARKETING MINIMALISM ADVANTAGE

Most experts overwhelm themselves with complex marketing systems because:

- They think more complexity equals more effectiveness
- They've been sold too many courses by too many gurus
- They're trying to copy consumer marketing approaches for B2B problems

The result? Marketing paralysis and funnel fatigue.

The reality is that for experts selling high-value solutions to businesses, simplicity isn't just easier. It's more effective.

FUNNEL #1: THE BOOK FUNNEL

Purpose: To build your list and authority while you sleep

This one is your inbound engine. It's simple, beautiful, and so damn leverageable.

Here's how it works:

- Someone clicks an ad or a link
- They land on a sexy, value-stacked page
- They opt in to get your book (free or $5 digital)
- They're added to your CRM
- They're offered an upsell (audio version, course preview, whatever)
- They're added to a nurture sequence
- You build the list and break even on ad spend

This is what we call a self-liquidating funnel.

WHY IT WORKS

- Everyone wants a book. It feels valuable.
- It positions you as the expert.
- It lets you sell without selling, because now you're the published authority
- The book becomes the doorway into your ecosystem

Don't have a book? Write one. 100–150 pages of value that solves a company-relevant problem.

Don't want to write one? Get us to help you.

Once it's built, it works 24/7, 365.

It doesn't just build your list.

It builds credibility, confidence, and inbound deal flow.

THE ANATOMY OF AN EFFECTIVE BOOK FUNNEL

Component	Purpose	Key Elements
Landing Page	Convert traffic to leads	Problem statement, book preview, strong CTA
Opt-in Form	Capture contact info	Name, email, qualifying question
Thank You Page	Deliver book & upsell	Download link, next-step offer
Initial Email	Immediate delivery	Book link, quick-win content
Nurture Sequence	Build relationship	Value-driven content, case studies, soft offers

The beauty of this funnel is its simplicity combined with its authority-building power. A book positions you differently than any other lead magnet could.

FUNNEL #2: THE VSL FUNNEL

Purpose: To qualify leads and fill your calendar with buyers

This one is the sales machine.

It replaces the discovery call. It filters out the tire kickers. It lets you scale 1:1 conversations without actually showing up.

Here's how it works:

- A lead clicks a link (from a post, ad, email, DM)
- They land on a page with a short Video Sales Letter (VSL), 3–10 minutes
- The video explains:

- The problem your audience has
- Why it's costing them
- Your approach to solving it
- What results look like
- Your offer suite and next steps
- Then there's a call-to-action to book a call
- They fill out a qualifying form (linked to your CRM)
- They book in, get reminders, and show up ready to buy

WHY IT WORKS

- You're selling with you, not a funnel that's impersonating you
- You control the narrative
- You warm up the lead before they hit your calendar
- You get qualified, serious buyers who already understand what you do

And because your CRM is tracking it all, your pipeline stays clean, visible, and cashflow-ready.

THE PERFECT VSL STRUCTURE

Your video sales letter doesn't need to be complex, but it does need to hit these points in order:

1. **Problem Identification (30 seconds):** "If you're struggling with X, Y, and Z..."

2. **Problem Amplification (60 seconds):** "This is costing you in these specific ways..."

3. **Solution Introduction (60-90 seconds):** "There's a better approach that works differently..."

4. **Your Method (60-90 seconds):** "Our system/ framework/program works by..."

5. **Proof Points (60-90 seconds):** "Companies like X and Y have seen these results..."

6. **Offer Overview (60 seconds):** "We have several ways we can help you..."

7. **Next Steps (30 seconds):** "Book a call to explore which option is right for you..."

The entire VSL should run 5-8 minutes, long enough to qualify, short enough to keep attention.

WHEN TO USE EACH FUNNEL

Funnel	Use It When...
Book Funnel	You want to build your list, warm leads
VSL Funnel	You want to book sales calls and close

Best part?

They can both run at the same time.

Book Funnel = Top of Funnel → Leads & Nurture VSL Funnel = Bottom of Funnel → Qualified Sales

You want both running?

You're building an Unsellable Empire.

THE TWO-FUNNEL ECOSYSTEM IN ACTION

Here's how these two simple funnels create a complete client acquisition machine:

Stage	Funnel	Purpose	Action
Awareness	Book	Attract interested prospects	LinkedIn/social ads to book page
Interest	Book	Establish expertise	Book delivery + value nurture
Consideration	Transition	Move from content to conversation	Nurture emails point to VSL
Intent	VSL	Qualify and educate	Video explains approach and options
Evaluation	VSL	Book qualified calls	Application form filters quality
Decision	Sales Call	Close deals	Present ecosystem options

This streamlined approach eliminates the need for complex funnels while still creating a complete customer journey.

HOW THEY CONNECT TO YOUR FLYWHEEL

This is where the ecosystem becomes electric.

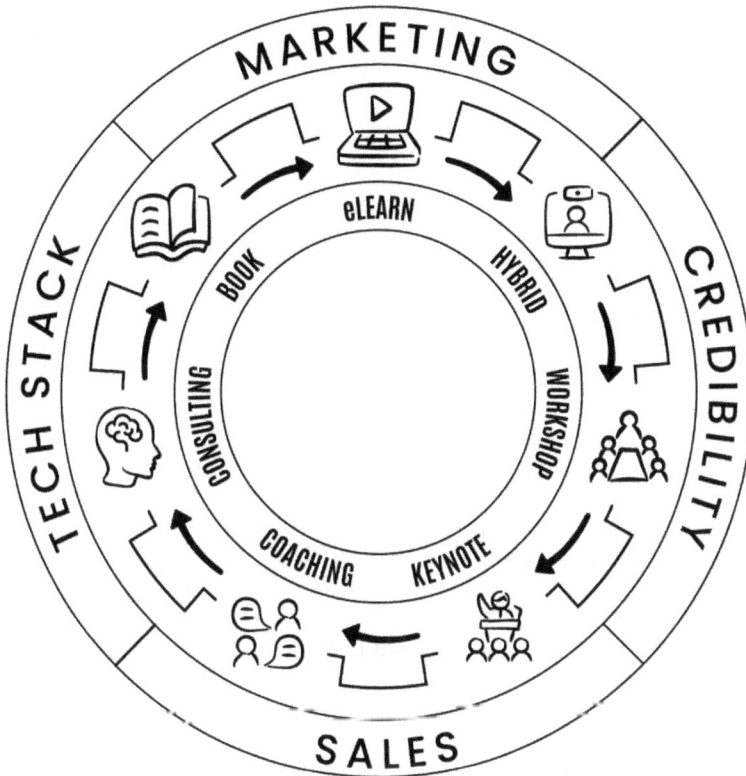

- Someone grabs your book → enters your world

- Your CRM sends nurture content

- They see your content on LinkedIn that builds credibility

- They watch your VSL

- They book a call

- You pitch the offer that suits their size, budget, and need

- You close.

- You deliver.

- You upsell later.

- The flywheel spins faster.

Implementation Timeline

You don't need to build both funnels at once. Here's a strategic approach:

Timing	Focus	Key Actions
Month 1	VSL Funnel	Create VSL script, record video, build landing page
Month 2	VSL Funnel	Set up calendar integration, CRM automation, qualifying form
Month 3	Book Funnel	Organise existing content or outline new book
Month 4	Book Funnel	Create landing page, thank you page, initial emails
Month 5	Integration	Connect both funnels, set up transition automations
Month 6	Optimisation	Test, refine, and scale what's working

Start with the VSL funnel if you need immediate sales conversations. Start with the Book funnel if you need to build authority and your audience. You could go faster if you want, we are here to help take it from 6 months to 6 days or 6 weeks if you want.

Once prospects move through these funnels, you'll need strong pricing and sales skills. Chapters 9-11 provide the frameworks you need to convert interested prospects into high-value clients.

IMPLEMENTATION STEPS

ONE BIG THING:

Choose which funnel to build first (Book or VSL) and create a 60-day build plan with weekly milestones.

Two Small Steps:

- Outline the content for your lead magnet (book) or VSL script
- Set up tracking to measure one key conversion point

🎧 BEYOND THE PAGE

Scan for Steve's unfiltered insights and implementation hacks in this chapter. (2-3 min)

Not the audiobook. Better.

CHAPTER 9:

HOW TO PRICE LIKE A WEAPONISED GENIUS

The Pricing Prison

"If you're solving a million-dollar problem and charging pennies, the issue isn't your clients' budget, it's your courage. Price for impact, not hours."

THE ESSENTIALS

- Price based on the value of the problem you solve, not hours worked

- Use the 10% Rule: charge 10% of the problem's cost or the value created

- Adopt the Elastic As F**k (EAF) approach to pricing across your ecosystem

- Add value multipliers that increase price without increasing your workload

- You're not expensive, you're solving expensive problems

CASE STUDY: OLIVIA - THE PRICING BREAKTHROUGH THAT TRIPLED REVENUE

BEFORE: Olivia saved clients millions and charged hourly like a mid-level contractor.

ACTION: We repositioned her pricing around outcomes, not hours. Packages started at $45k and scaled to $250k.

AFTER:

- Doubled her annual revenue

- Attracted better clients faster

"I was pricing time, not value. Now I charge for transformation."

Let's cut the shit.

Most experts are chronically undercharging, and it's not because they're bad.

It's because they're still doing maths based on time.

"What's my hourly rate?" "How long will it take me?" "What's the market price for this?"

WRONG QUESTIONS.

You're not selling minutes. You're selling meaningful, measurable outcomes.

This chapter is your upgrade.

This is how you stop being a time-for-money expert and start being an outcome-driven profit printer.

THE TIME-VALUE TRAP

When you price based on time, you create three devastating problems:

1. **Income Ceiling:** You can only make as much as your hours allow

2. **Value Disconnect:** The client focuses on your time, not their transformation

3. **Expertise Penalty:** The faster you solve problems, the less you earn

This trap keeps talented experts stuck in a perpetual hustle, constantly trading life for money with no way to scale.

THE EAF PRICING APPROACH: A TRUE STORY

Meet Julianne.

She was a brilliant change management expert who came to us confused about pricing.

"I just billed a Fortune 500 client $15K for my workshop, then charged a startup $12K for basically the same thing. Something feels off."

I asked about what each client was solving.

"The Fortune 500 is rolling out an ERP system. If employees resist, they'll lose about $2M in productivity."

"And the startup?"

"Toxic team dynamics causing developer exodus. They've lost three senior devs at $30K each in replacement costs. Two more, and they miss funding milestones."

"So," I said, "you charged 0.75% of the problem value to the Fortune 500 and about 13% to the startup?"

The realisation hit her. "I'm massively undercharging the big client."

This is where most experts freak out:

- "But it's the same workshop!"
- "It's the same hours!"
- "They'll never pay more for the same thing!"

This is where you need to embrace the Elastic As F**k approach to pricing.

THE EAF PRICING MINDSET

Your pricing needs to be elastic as f**k. Not rigid. Not fixed. Not even consistent across clients.

TL;DR: In economics, when something is highly elastic, it means it's extremely variable and responsive to conditions. Your pricing needs to be the same, completely flexible, and responsive to the value of each specific problem you're solving.

The truth: The value of a solution has nothing to do with the format or time it takes to deliver.

A 90-minute workshop preventing a $1M disaster? Worth $100K. A year-long consulting engagement solving a $50K problem? Worth $5K.

Stop thinking of your ecosystem as a fixed-price menu and start thinking of it as a flexible set of solutions, each priced according to the specific value it creates for each specific client.

Yes, you can anchor each cog with a "FROM:" price for your own sanity:

- Self-Directed eLearn: FROM $10K
- Workshop: FROM $5K
- Consulting: FROM $40K

But that's just to keep you from going mental. It's not a ceiling or even a guideline.

This EAF approach gives you three massive advantages:

1. **No More Pricing Ceilings:** Your workshop isn't "worth" $10K. It's worth 10% of whatever problem it solves. **Freedom From Formats:** Stop thinking, "I can only charge X for a workshop," and start thinking, "This solution is worth Y because it solves a Z-sized problem." **Client-Specific Confidence:** Quote $50K for an eLearn with complete confidence because you know it's solving a $500K problem for that specific client. When clients say, "That seems expensive for an online program," you calmly reply:

"You mentioned this problem is costing you about $400K annually. We're solving it for $40K. That's a 10x return. Does that feel like good value?"

Then, watch as they nod and reach for their corporate card.

FIRST RULE: VALUE-BASED PRICING ONLY

If you remember one thing from this book, let it be this:

Price your offer based on the cost of the problem you solve.

Let's say your program helps improve manager capability in a company that's bleeding talent.

That retention problem?

- Let's say 20 staff quit each year
- Average cost per exit = $25k
- Total = $500,000/year problem

If your hybrid training solves even 20% of that problem, that's $100,000 in savings.

So charging $20–40k for that solution?

Not only is that fair, it's generous.

THE VALUE CALCULATION FRAMEWORK

To establish value-based pricing, you need to quantify the problem. Here's how:

Problem Type	Calculation Approach	Example
Cost Problems	Direct costs × Frequency	20 staff leaving × $25k per exit = $500k
Time Problems	Hours saved × Hourly value	5,000 hours saved × $50/hr = $250k
Revenue Problems	Conversion lift × Revenue value	2% lift × $5M pipeline = $100k
Risk Problems	Probability × Cost of incident	15% chance × $1M liability = $150k

Once you've quantified the problem, your price becomes a simple fraction of that value.

THE EXPERT MATH EQUATION

Here's your pricing logic in one sexy formula:

Cost of the Problem × 10% = Your Price

OR

Gain from the Outcome × 10% = Your Price

If your solution saves $1 million → Price it at $100k If your solution helps them gain $200k → Price it at $20k

This is how grown-up B2B companies price. This is how you justify your fee to CFOs, not just feelings.

THE T-SHIRT SIZE MODEL AS A STARTING STRUCTURE

To give yourself some initial structure while embracing the EAF approach, the T-Shirt Size Model can be helpful:

Size	What It Could Include	EAF Approach
S	Self-directed only (off-the-shelf)	10% of the specific problem value
M	Self-directed + branding	10% of the specific problem value +10% premium
L	Hybrid program + light customisation	10% of the specific problem value + 15-20% premium
XL	Fully custom experience	10% of the specific problem value + 20-30% premium

The beauty of this model is that an S offering could be $5K or $50K, depending on the problem value. An XL could be $25K or $250K. It's EAF. I can already feel some of you hyper-analytical cats going, "What about x?" All good. EAF remember.

You sell it based on need. You stack value. You never discount. You redirect to a different size that delivers appropriate value for their budget.

This T-shirt sizing approach integrates perfectly with the sales techniques in Chapters 10 and 11, giving you a clear structure to present options during sales conversations.

WHAT DRIVES PRICE UP (WITHOUT EXTRA WORK)

Want to charge more without adding time?

- Customisation (branding, logos, language)
- Inclusion of data/reporting
- Access to you (live calls, check-ins, coaching)
- Duration (12-month license vs one-off delivery)
- Number of seats (scale = value = $$$)
- Internal comms support (we'll even help them roll it out)

You're not selling features. You're selling a smoother path to the result. That's what clients pay more for.

VALUE MULTIPLIERS MATRIX

The right value additions can double or triple your price with minimal additional work:

Multiplier	Value to Client	Work for You	Price Impact
Multi-year license	Long-term solution	None after setup	Can charge more
Enterprise roll-out	Company-wide impact	Minimal	More users can charge more
Executive access	High-level insights	Limited hours	Extra work for you, can charge more

Implementation support	Faster adoption	Structured process	Hands on support, you can charge more
Exclusive IP	Competitive advantage	None	Custom work = custom price

The key is adding elements that dramatically increase client value while requiring minimal additional effort from you.

You're Not Expensive. You're Experienced.

Let's say it louder for the experts at the back:

Price is a reflection of belief. Margin is a reflection of leadership. Profit is a reflection of discipline.

You're not charging for your time. You're charging for:

- The result
- The efficiency
- The certainty
- The IP you spent years refining
- The peace of mind they get when you're in the room

That's priceless. But we're generous, so we'll put a number on it.

COMMUNICATING VALUE WITHOUT APOLOGISING

When discussing price, use these value-anchoring statements:

Instead of	Say This
"Our price is…"	"The investment for this solution is…"
"This costs…"	"For a $500k problem, we solve it for…"

"We charge..."	"Companies typically invest..."
"That's our rate"	"That reflects the scale of impact we deliver"
"I can discount if needed"	"We have other options at different investment levels"

Notice how each reframe shifts from cost to value, from expense to investment.

IMPLEMENTATION STEPS

ONE BIG THING:

Calculate the actual cost of the problem you solve for clients and apply the 10% rule to establish your baseline pricing.

Two Small Steps:

- Practice saying your highest prices out loud until they feel comfortable
- List 3 value-adds you could include that require minimal extra work from you

🎧 BEYOND THE PAGE

Scan for Steve's unfiltered insights and implementation hacks in this chapter. (2-3 min)

Not the audiobook. Better.

CHAPTER 10:

SALES THAT DON'T FEEL GROSS

The Expert's Sales Mindset

"Nobody likes a desperate salesperson. Everyone respects a confident problem solver. Be the second one and watch your conversion rate soar." — Steve Corney

THE ESSENTIALS

- Selling is helping people make confident decisions about solving their problems
- Anchor to the cost of the problem, not your time or effort
- Embrace the EAF approach across your entire ecosystem
- Never discount, redirect to a more appropriate offering instead
- Use your ecosystem to handle objections without compromising value

CASE STUDY: DAVID - FROM SALES ANXIETY TO CONFIDENT CLOSING

BEFORE: David, a cybersecurity genius, froze every time money came up in sales conversations.

ACTION: We reframed sales as solving massive risk problems, not "asking for money."

AFTER:

- Closed a $75k contract immediately
- Jumped close rates from 20% to 45%

"I wasn't selling I was solving."

Sales.

That one word that makes every expert suddenly feel like a used car dealer on a coke bender.

But here's the truth: You're offering real solutions to real problems that are costing companies real money.

That's not sales. That's leadership.

And if you can't communicate your value, you'll stay in the "broke genius" category, while less talented people make more money than you because they weren't afraid to ask for the cheque.

THE VALUE-CONVICTION DISCONNECT

Most experts struggle with sales for one simple reason: They believe in their expertise, but they don't believe in their right to be paid well for it.

This creates a disconnect where you:

- Deliver transformational value
- But charge transactional prices

This isn't just a mindset issue. It's a business killer.

THE BIG LIE: "IF I'M GOOD ENOUGH, THEY'LL JUST BUY"

No, they won't. They're too busy and distracted to notice your brilliance without your help.

If you don't own the sales conversation, you'll lose to someone who does.

So from now on, this is the rule: **Selling = Helping people make a confident decision about solving their problem with you.**

Reframing the Sales Conversation

The moment you shift from "selling your stuff" to "solving their problem," everything changes:

Old Frame	New Frame
"I need this sale"	"They need this solution"

"Am I worth this price?"	"Is solving this problem worth this price?"
"I hope they say yes"	"Let's see if we're a good fit"
"What if they reject me?"	"What if I can help them avoid costly mistakes?"

This isn't manipulation, it's perspective, the difference between begging and leading.

THE MENTAL FLIP: PRICE = CONFIDENCE

Here's the deal:

- If you charge $500, they'll treat it like $500.

- If you charge $50k, they'll pull up a chair and take notes.

The higher your price, the more seriously they'll take you, as long as you can anchor that price to the value you deliver.

Learn to say it like this: "This program is $40,000. You're trying to fix a retention problem that's costing you $500,000 a year. If we fix even 10% of that, we're ahead. Make sense?"

THE UNSELLABLE SALES STACK

1. **Have a Clear Offer Suite:** Know your flywheel. Know your cogs. Be ready to flex up and down based on client needs while maintaining elastic pricing tied to problem value.

2. **Anchor to the Problem, Not the Product:** "You said retention is your #1 challenge. Our hybrid program helps managers spot at-risk staff before they walk. Here's how it works.

"That's how pros talk.

1. **Handle Budget Objections with the EAF Approach:** When they say, "We don't have budget," you say:

"Let's look at what the problem is costing you. If we can solve a $200K problem for $20K, does that create room in the budget?"

Or: "What budget do you have available? We can configure a solution that solves the highest-value aspects of the problem within your constraints."

Flex the offer, not your value.

2. **Use the Ecosystem to Navigate Budget Realities:** They say "no" to consulting? Here's a workshop. Too much? Here's a self-directed program. Still too early? Grab the book.

You never lose the sale. You just move it to a different cog within your ecosystem.

To see exactly how to structure these sales conversations step-by-step, continue to Chapter 11, where we break down the PACER framework.

THE ELASTIC VALUE LADDER IN ACTION

Your ecosystem provides multiple entry points for clients, each priced according to the value of the problem it solves— not the hours you put in.

Entry Point	Primary Value	Elastic Pricing Approach
Book/Resource	Introduces your thinking and approach	Most accessible entry point
Self-Directed eLearn	Delivers your IP at scale across teams	10% of the problem it solves

Hybrid Program	Blends automation with live expertise	10% of the problem it solves
Workshop	Creates focused transformation	10% of the problem it solves
Keynote	Builds awareness and credibility	Strategic visibility investment
Coaching	Provides personalised implementation	10% of the problem it solves
Consulting	Offers comprehensive expertise access	10% of the problem it solves

Your ecosystem isn't about fixed price points. It's about value relationships.

A consulting engagement that solves a $50K problem may cost $5K for a report, whereas a self-directed eLearn that solves a $1 million organisational issue may cost $100K. It's not about the delivery method. It is all about the problem's value.

Each offering in your ecosystem adheres to the 10% rule from Chapter 9: price at roughly 10% of the problem value or outcome delivered. This makes your pricing Elastic As F**k. Any cog in your flywheel can cost anywhere from a few thousand dollars to hundreds of thousands, depending on the size and impact of the problem it solves.

The offerings do not follow a fixed price hierarchy. They're in a value-delivery relationship. Sometimes, a workshop may provide more immediate value than a consulting engagement. Sometimes, an eLearn has more organisation-wide impact than a coaching program.

This elasticity is your competitive advantage. It lets you meet clients where they are with the right solution, priced according to value, not time or delivery method.

MAKE IT EASY TO SAY YES

Use a one-pager for every offer that reinforces the value-based, elastic pricing approach:

1. **The Problem:** "You're facing [specific challenge] which is costing you [quantified impact]"

2. **The Solution:** "Our [program name] solves this by [core approach]"

3. **The Proof:** "We've helped [similar companies] achieve [specific results]"

4. **The Value Relationship:** "For a problem costing $X, our solution investment is $Y, creating a Z× return"

5. **The Next Step:** One clear call to action

Remember: Always tie the investment back to the problem value, not to the delivery method. This reinforces that you're not selling "a workshop" or "an eLearn." You're selling a solution to a specific, costly problem.

THE IMPACT-TO-INVESTMENT RATIO

When discussing solutions, use this simple formula to reinforce the value relationship: **Client Impact ÷ Your Price = Value Multiplier**

Solution Example	Client Problem Value	Your Price	Value Multiplier
eLearn Program	$500,000 issue	$50,000	10× return
Workshop Series	$300,000 challenge	$30,000	10× return
Consulting	$2M opportunity	$200,000	10× return

Notice how the delivery method varies, but the value relationship remains consistent. This is the EAF approach in action. The price scales with the problem value, not the delivery format.

IMPLEMENTATION STEPS

ONE BIG THING:

Reframe your offerings as solutions to specific, quantifiable problems with clear value multipliers.

Two Small Steps:

- Draft responses to budget objections that redirect to value, not discounts
- Create a one-page "problem-solution-value" template for your primary offering

🎧 BEYOND THE PAGE

Scan for Steve's unfiltered insights and implementation hacks on this chapter. (2-3 min)

Not the audiobook. Better.

CHAPTER 11:

THE PACER SALES CONVERSATION FRAMEWORK

The Diagnostic Approach

"Stop pitching and start diagnosing. When you ask better questions than anyone else, you don't need to sell, they ask to buy."

THE ESSENTIALS

- Use PACER: Problem, Amplify, Clarify, Explain, Redirect/ Recommend
- Diagnose before you prescribe, understand their problems deeply
- Make the cost of inaction clear to establish value context for EAF pricing
- Present solutions mapped specifically to their revealed needs
- Master each step of the framework for natural, non-pushy selling

CASE STUDY: GRACE - THE FRAMEWORK THAT TURNED COURTESY CALLS INTO CONTRACTS

BEFORE: Grace had discovery calls, but prospects ghosted after.

ACTION: We installed the PACER framework combined with the EAF pricing approach.

AFTER:

- Increased conversion rate from 12% to 35%
- Closed $40k deals she used to lose

> *"I was proving my expertise when I should have been proving my understanding."*

Let's paint the scene:

You're on a call. Someone's interested. They booked through your funnel. They downloaded your book. They follow you on

LinkedIn.

Now what? This is where most experts crumble.

Why? Because they think the sales call is about performing. It's not. It's about diagnosing.

You're not here to be impressive. You're here to ask the right questions, identify the real problem, quantify its cost, and show them how you solve it.

THE EXPERT'S SALES CONVERSATION DILEMMA

Most experts talk too much about their methods instead of diagnosing the client's actual problem. They dive into their methodology, credentials, and process before they understand what the client truly needs.

The result? Fascinating conversations that go nowhere.

THE PACER FRAMEWORK: STEP BY STEP

We call it PACER. It's fast, fluid, and gets to the real issues without ever feeling like a pitch. It's also the perfect vehicle for implementing the Elastic As F**k pricing approach.

This framework builds directly on the pricing principles from Chapter 9 and the sales mindset from Chapter 10, creating a complete sales system for your expert business.

PROBLEM

"What's going on in your business right now that brought you to this call?"

This is where you shut up and let them talk. Don't sell. Don't jump in. Don't fix. Let them show you what's broken.

Problem-Seeking Questions:

Surface Problem	Deeper Question	Real Issue
"Teamconflict"	"How is that affecting delivery?"	Performance gaps
"Highturnover"	"Which roles are you losing most?"	Leadership deficiency
"Change resistance"	"What happens when you try to implement?"	Trust breakdown

Your goal: Get to the problem behind the problem—the one they're actually willing to pay to solve.

Pro tip: At this stage, you're not just identifying the problem. You're laying the groundwork for quantifying its value, which is essential for EAF pricing.

AMPLIFY

"And if this keeps going the way it is, what's the impact?"

Now we stir the pot. Get into the cost of the problem:

- **Current Costs:** "How much is this costing you right now?"

- **Future Costs:** "What happens if this continues for another year?"

- **Opportunity Costs:** "What could you be doing instead if this was solved?"

- **Personal Costs:** "How is this affecting you as a leader?"

This is the critical step for EAF pricing. You need to quantify the problem so your price can be properly calibrated to its value. Remember: you are paid in proportion to the size of the problem you solve. So, make it real. Make it felt. Make it cost something.

If you skip this step, you can't implement EAF pricing effectively.

Value Amplification Questions:

Problem Type	Amplification Question	Quantification Goal
Performance issues	"What does this cost in productivity?"	$ per hour × hours lost
Retention problems	"What's your cost to replace someone?"	Replacement cost × turnover rate
Client experience issues	"How does this affect client lifetime value?"	Revenue impact per client × clients affected
Implementation delays	"What's the cost of each month of delay?"	Monthly cost × anticipated delay

The bigger and more concrete they perceive the problem, the more valuable your solution becomes, and the more you can charge using the EAF approach.

CLARIFY THE DESIRED STATE

"What would things look like if this was solved?"

Let them dream a little. They're stressed. They're overwhelmed. They don't want a course. They want clarity. They want the after state.

Help them paint a detailed picture of success:

- What metrics would improve?
- How would people behave differently?
- What would leaders be able to focus on instead?
- What would the day-to-day experience feel like?

The more vivid their vision of the solution, the more urgent their desire to achieve it—and the more open they'll be to your elastic pricing approach when you present it.

EXPLAIN THE ECOSYSTEM

Now, and only now, do you show your cards.

"Okay, based on what you've shared, here's how we typically approach this kind of problem."

This is your flywheel moment. Show them the options in your ecosystem that directly address the problems they've just revealed to you. Be sure to tie each option back to the value it creates, not to its format or the time it takes to deliver.

When explaining your solution, follow this EAF-influenced structure:

1. **Problem Value Recap:** "You mentioned this issue is costing about $500K annually..."

2. **Solution Approach:** "Our approach to solving this has generated 80% improvement in similar situations..."

3. **Value-Based Options:** "We have several ways to help, each priced according to the value it creates..."

4. **Implementation Path:** "The typical rollout looks like this..."

5. **Expected Results:** "Based on similar implementations, you should see ROI within X months..."

Notice how the focus remains on value, not on feature comparison or time-based pricing.

REDIRECT OR RECOMMEND

"Given what we've discussed, here's what I recommend."

Now you guide. You either:

- Recommend the right option based on the problem value you've established
- Present your solution using the 10% rule from Chapter 9
- Offer alternatives if their budget constraints require it
- Then say: "Does that approach make sense given what we've discussed?"

And then: shut up. Let them speak. Let them buy. If you've done this right, they already have.

Remember, as we discussed in Chapter 10, your ecosystem offers multiple entry points, each priced according to the value of the problem it solves, not its delivery format. This gives you incredible flexibility in this final stage of the conversation.

EAF PRICING IN ACTION DURING THE PACER FRAMEWORK

Here's how EAF pricing integrates into each step of PACER:

PACER Stage	EAF Application
Problem	Identify issues that have quantifiable business impact
Amplify	Establish concrete value/cost of the problem

Clarify	Create desire for solutions worth paying for
Explain	Connect solutions to problem value, not delivery method
Redirect/ Recommend	Price at 10% of problem value, regardless of format

THE ELASTIC SOLUTIONS MATRIX

Each objection or hesitation has a specific ecosystem solution, all priced elastically based on problem value:

Common Friction Point	EAF Solution Approach	Why It Works
"It's too expensive"	"Let's revisit the problem value"	Re-anchors to value, not price
"We need to test first"	"Let's start with a focused solution to your highest-value problem"	Creates proof point at appropriate scale
"We need proof it works"	"Here's how we've solved similar $X problems for $Y"	Shows value relationship precedent
"Too many initiatives now"	"Let's solve the most costly issue first"	Prioritises based on problem value
"Need executive buy-in"	"Let's quantify the full cost for leadership"	Creates compelling business case

Your ecosystem's elasticity is your greatest objection handler, letting you configure solutions that create 10× return regardless of client budget or readiness level.

OPTIONAL CLOSER: "WOULD YOU LIKE OUR HELP?"

No pressure. No pitch. Just this:

"It sounds like we could really help you solve this $X problem for about $Y, creating a 10× return. Would you like our help with that?"

Notice how the closing question keeps the focus on the value relationship, not the price itself.

The Follow-Through Process

After the call, maintain momentum with value-focused follow-up:

1. **Same Day:** Send a one-pager showing problem value and solution investment

2. **1-2 Days:** If no response, send a voice note or short video reinforcing the cost of inaction

3. **3-4 Days:** Share a relevant case study showing similar value created

4. **5-7 Days:** Final check-in with a specific question about problem impact

5. **Weekly:** Add to nurture sequence focused on problem awareness and quantification

Remember: Your goal isn't to close every deal; it's to maintain relationships with quality prospects who will buy when the time is right and at prices that reflect the true value of the problems you solve.

IMPLEMENTATION STEPS

ONE BIG THING:

Practice the "Amplify" stage by role-playing how to help clients calculate and feel the full cost of their problem.

Two Small Steps:

- Script 3-5 problem quantification questions for your specific expertise area
- Create a simple value calculation template you can use during sales conversations

🎧 BEYOND THE PAGE

Scan for Steve's unfiltered insights and implementation hacks on this chapter. (2-3 min)

Not the audiobook. Better.

IV

PROTECTION & LIFESTYLE

"A business that devours its creator isn't a success, it's a tragedy. True mastery is building a fortress around your genius that protects both your intellectual property and your quality of life."

CHAPTER 12:

LIVING THE UNSELLABLE LIFE

The Revolution Realised

"Success isn't building something you can flog off to the highest bidder. It's building something so bloody perfect you'd never want to part with it."

THE ESSENTIALS

- The Unsellable Life means building a high-margin, purpose-driven business
- Your business should be built on you while not being dependent on you
- Focus on profit per hour worked rather than total revenue
- Curate your clients, projects, and time instead of accepting everything
- Real success is having the freedom to work on your terms

CASE STUDY: TOM - FROM SUCCESS TO SIGNIFICANCE

BEFORE: Tom built a seven-figure consulting business, and felt trapped in it. He didn't want to sell. He wanted to reconnect with meaningful work.

ACTION: We restructured everything around selective, high-impact engagements and true personal brand alignment.

AFTER:

- Increased profits by 15%
- Reignited passion for the work

"I'm doing less volume but more meaningful work and I'd never want to sell it."

Take a breath. Look around.

You've built the ecosystem. You've built the offers. You've built the machine. And you've built it around you.

No investors. No cofounders. No 60-person team. No bullshit.

Just your expertise, your systems, your integrity, and a business that fits into a backpack if it needs to.

Welcome to the Unsellable Life.

BEYOND BUSINESS: THE UNSELLABLE PHILOSOPHY

What we've built together isn't just a business model. It's a life philosophy.

A rejection of:

- Growth for growth's sake
- Other people's definitions of success
- The false choice between impact and freedom
- The pressure to exit, scale, or conform

And an embrace of:

- Intentional design of work and life
- Value-based wealth creation
- Expertise as your greatest leverage
- Building something that serves you first

This isn't just about money. It's about reclaiming what success actually means.

WHAT THIS LOOKS LIKE IN THE REAL WORLD

Let's break it down.

You've got:

- A self-directed eLearn that's been licensed to 10 companies at $30k/year = $300k

- A few hybrid workshops scheduled across the year = $50–100k
- A dozen keynotes at $5k a pop = $60k
- Some advisory or consulting retainers for high-leverage projects = $60–100k
- Maybe some group coaching or cohort training to stay sharp = $20–50k
- And a book that feeds it all = leads daily, credibility everywhere

That's $500k–$600k+ a year doing work that lights you up.

No funnels to fix. No random 1:1 calls to squeeze in. Just quality output, leveraged delivery, and high-margin work.

THE METRICS THAT MATTER

In the Unsellable model, we measure success differently:

Traditional Metrics	Unsellable Metrics
Revenue growth	Profit per hour worked
Team size	Impact per client
Market share	Category ownership
Recurring revenue	Work/life alignment
Capital raised	Peace of mind

It's a fundamental shift from chasing more to creating better, in both business and life.

You're Not Hustling. You're Curating.

You choose:

- Which clients to work with
- Which months to take off
- Which part of your ecosystem to amplify
- Which platform to show up on
- Which stage you want to be on next

You're not responding to demand. You're orchestrating it.

And because your offers are productised, the whole thing is scalable:

You can:

- Add facilitators
- License your content
- Run more ads
- Build a team, or not
- Bolt on events, community, masterminds, or IP deals

You're not stuck anymore.

THE CURATION FRAMEWORK

The power to choose is the ultimate freedom. Here's how to exercise it:

Decision Area	Low Value	High Value
Clients	Difficult, price-sensitive, energy-draining	Collaborative, value-focused, energising

Projects	Customised one-offs	Repeatable, leverageable assets
Time	Scattered, reactive	Blocked, themed, protected
Platform	Chasing trends	Owning your space
Growth	Linear (more hours)	Exponential (better systems)

Curation isn't about doing less. It's about doing better.

THE REAL FLEX: PEACE, SPACE, PURPOSE

Let's talk about the stuff that matters.

- You wake up without panic
- You know where your next clients are coming from
- You're not stressing over rent
- You're building assets while others are building hourly invoices
- You're able to travel, think, rest, create, breathe
- You're not chasing relevance, you own your category

You're not famous. You're free. You're not viral. You're valuable. You're not exhausted. You're energized.

That's the Unsellable life.

THE INVISIBLE BENEFITS

Beyond the obvious perks, the Unsellable life delivers deeper rewards:

- **Mental Bandwidth:** Space to think and create at a higher level

- **Relationship Depth:** Quality time for the people who matter
- **Health Recovery:** Energy for self-care and wellness
- **Creative Expansion:** Freedom to explore new ideas and directions
- **Legacy Construction:** Building something that outlasts your direct involvement

These aren't luxuries. They're the foundations of a life well-lived.

This lifestyle is only possible with the solid foundations built through the ecosystem (Chapter 4), strategic building approach (Chapter 5), and proper tech infrastructure (Chapter 6).

You Built This. With What You Already Had.

Not some lottery idea. Not some bullshit trend.

You took what you already knew, packaged it smarter, sold it cleaner, and delivered it with intention.

You didn't sell your soul for scale. You didn't chase investors. You didn't pretend to be something you weren't.

You just doubled down on what made you valuable and turned it into velocity.

FROM PRACTITIONER TO ARCHITECT

The journey from expert to Unsellable business owner is a profound evolution:

Phase	Focus	Mindset	Primary Activity
Practitioner	Doing the work	"I need clients"	Direct delivery

Professional	Improving the work	"I need systems"	Process refinement
Producer	Packaging the work	"I need products"	IP development
Proprietor	Leveraging the work	"I need scale"	Strategic growth
Pioneer	Transcending the work	"I need impact"	Movement building

Each phase builds on the last, with the Unsellable model accelerating your progress.

THIS LIFE IS AVAILABLE TO ANYONE... BUT NOT FOR FREE

Here's the truth:

You don't "fall into" the Unsellable Life. You build it. Intentionally. Strategically. One cog at a time.

If you want this life, the blueprint's right here. This book is your map. The Expert Ecosystem is your engine.

So here's your only question: What are you going to do next?

YOUR NEXT 90 DAYS

The journey of a thousand miles begins with a single step. Here's your roadmap:

1. **Days 1–30:** Inventory your current IP and offerings
2. **Days 31–60:** Choose your next cog and create your mock-up
3. **Days 61–90:** Pre-sell to one client and start building

Don't overwhelm yourself. Don't try to build everything at once.

Start with what you have. Move to what's next. Trust the process.

IMPLEMENTATION STEPS

ONE BIG THING:

Define what "success" looks like for you beyond financial metrics and schedule your ideal work calendar.

Two Small Steps:

- Identify your first "no" - one type of client or project you'll start declining
- Block time in your calendar this week for rest, thinking, and strategic work

🎧 BEYOND THE PAGE

Scan for Steve's unfiltered insights and implementation hacks in this chapter. (2-3 min)

Not the audiobook. Better.

CHAPTER 13:

PROTECTING YOUR IP WITHOUT PARANOIA

The Protection Paradox

"If you're hiding your best ideas, you're robbing yourself twice—first of impact, then of income. Protect the core, share the rest, and keep moving."

THE ESSENTIALS

- Focus protection on what matters most: branded frameworks, signature programs
- Copyright automatically protects your expression; consider trademarks for key elements
- B2C markets pose higher IP theft risk than B2B clients
- Document creation dates and ownership for everything important
- Your best protection is continuous innovation, stay ahead of the copycats

CASE STUDY: JENNIFER - THE BALANCE BETWEEN PROTECTION AND PARALYSIS

BEFORE: Jennifer feared having her IP stolen so much that she limited her own growth.

ACTION: We protected her key assets, structured licensing deals, and helped her scale safely.

AFTER:

- Removed her fear and blockers
- Confidently put her best work out into the world
- Not a single thing stolen
- Added $200k+ in new revenue from licensing deals

> *"I was so afraid of theft, I was stealing from myself."*

Let's have the conversation most experts avoid:

What if someone steals your shit?

It's real. It's valid. It's happened.

But here's the thing:

Fear of theft kills more dreams than theft ever has.

Yes, you need to protect your work.

But not by hiding in a cave, clutching your PDFs like Gollum, and whispering "my precious."

You protect your IP by building smarter, documenting better, and understanding the actual law, not the made-up guru bullshit.

Let's unpack it.

THE HIDDEN COST OF IP PARANOIA

Many experts never launch their best work because they're paralysed by fear:

- Fear their ideas will be stolen
- Fear their content will be copied
- Fear they'll lose control of what they've created

This paranoia leads to:

- Vague marketing that doesn't clearly communicate value
- Withholding your best insights until after purchase
- Refusing to license or share your work with organisations
- Creating unnecessarily complex content to prevent copying

The result? Your best work never sees the light of day, and you sabotage your own impact.

This balanced approach to IP protection complements the strategic building process covered in Chapter 5, protecting what matters while still getting your work into the world.

UNDERSTANDING THE BASICS

Here's what every expert needs to know:

Trademark

- Protects names, logos, slogans, visual models
- You apply for this (nationally or globally)
- Super helpful if you want to own a category or model

Example: "The Limitless Manager™" → Trademarked title and visual model

Copyright

- Protects your expression (videos, text, images, courses, eLearns, slides)
- Automatically yours when you create it
- You don't need to register it
- But you DO need to prove it was yours first if shit goes down

Example: Someone copies your eLearn word for word = copyright infringement. Someone paraphrases your framework? Probably not.

IDEAS VS. EXPRESSION: THE CRITICAL DISTINCTION

Understanding this fundamental principle changes how you approach IP protection:

What's Protected	What's Not Protected
The specific expression of an idea	The general idea itself

Your exact words, images, videos	Concepts, methodologies, approaches
Your unique arrangement of content	General frameworks and principles
Your branded terminology	Generic industry terms

This distinction liberates you to share your expertise widely while protecting the specific expressions that represent your unique value.

INTELLECTUAL PROPERTY PROTECTION HIERARCHY

Different types of content warrant different levels of protection:

Protection Level	Content Type	Protection Method
High Priority	Brand names, program titles, signature frameworks	Trademark registration
Medium Priority	Course structure, unique methodologies, visual models	Copyright notices, documentation
Low Priority	General ideas, industry concepts, universal principles	Focus on execution, not protection

Focus your protection efforts on what's truly distinctive and valuable in your business.

SO... HOW DO YOU ACTUALLY PROTECT YOUR SHIT?

1. **Document Everything:** Keep versions. Dates. Emails. Drafts. When in doubt, send your work to yourself or a friend for time-stamping.

2. **Use Video:** This is why we love self-directed eLearns.

You can't "accidentally" steal a professionally produced video. You can copy words. You can't easily rip 15 chapters of video, motion graphics, and embedded activities.

3. **Add Disclaimers:** Every course, workshop, proposal, or keynote deck should have this: "All content is © [Your Name/Company]. No part of this program may be reproduced or distributed without written permission." Simple. Effective. It makes people think twice.

4. **Send Contracts with Licensing Terms:** Especially when delivering on a company's LMS. "License valid for X staff for 12 months. Additional users beyond this require a new agreement." Boom. You're now protected and professional.

PRACTICAL PROTECTION STRATEGIES BY OFFERING

Different offerings in your ecosystem require different protection approaches:

Offering	Protection Strategy	Implementation
Book	Copyright notice, distinctive visual style	Include copyright page, unique layout and design
Workshop	Licensing agreements, watermarked materials	Clear terms for materials, post-workshop usage guidelines
eLearn	Technical protection, usage tracking	Platform security, user authentication, access limits

Keynote	Registration of key visuals, clear usage terms	Trademark visual models, licensing for recording
Consulting	Confidentiality agreements, phased deliverables	NDAs, strategic phasing of sensitive IP

Protection isn't just legal. It's built into how you design, deliver, and distribute your offerings.

THE REAL THREAT ISN'T CORPORATES

We've helped build and launch over 100 expert programs.

Guess who tries to steal IP the most? Other experts Wannabe coaches The B2C lurkers buying your $99 program to "reverse engineer" it.

Big businesses don't steal. They've got too much to lose: reputation, press, legal costs, brand damage. And they've got a budget. They don't need to rip your content. They just want to know you're legit, scalable, and safe to work with.

UNDERSTANDING THE COPYCAT MENTALITY

The psychology of copycats reveals why corporate clients are rarely the threat:

Copycat Type	Motivation	Threat Level	Best Defense
Industry Peers	Status, shortcuts, competitive pressure	Medium–High	Public attribution, distinctive delivery style

Entry-Level Coaches	Lacking original IP, seeking shortcuts	High	Format diversification, relationship building
B2C Bargain Hunters	Trying to "crack the code" without paying	Medium	Tiered access, progressive disclosure
Corporate Clients	Solving specific problems for their teams	Very Low	Professional licensing, trusted relationships

Understanding who might copy you helps you protect the right things in the right ways.

THE BIGGER TRUTH: YOU CAN'T CONTROL COPYCATS- BUT YOU CAN OUTRUN THEM

Someone rips your model? You're already three programs ahead.

Someone takes your concept? Your format, your voice, your delivery, and your credibility can't be copied.

Let them chase shadows. You keep building the real thing.

THE VELOCITY ADVANTAGE

The best protection is acceleration. Here's why:

1. **Market Leadership:** Being first and best creates perceived ownership
2. **Relationship Depth:** Genuine connections can't be copied
3. **Continuous Innovation:** Always be developing your next offering

4. **Public Attribution:** Regular visibility creates association with your IP

5. **Delivery Excellence:** How you implement matters more than what you teach

The most successful experts aren't those with the strongest legal protection. They're those who innovate faster than copycats can steal.

The Expert's IP Protection Checklist

Before launching any new offering, run through this quick protection checklist:

1. Have you documented the development process?

2. Are your key brand elements trademarked?

3. Do all materials include proper copyright notices?

4. Do your client agreements include IP protection clauses?

5. Have you diversified your content formats?

6. Is your unique voice and perspective clearly established?

7. Do you have a response plan if copying occurs?

You don't need perfect protection, just enough to deter casual theft and build a foundation for action if needed.

IMPLEMENTATION STEPS

ONE BIG THING:

Identify the 3-5 most valuable IP assets in your business and document their development history.

Two Small Steps:

- Add proper copyright notices to all your materials
- Create simple licensing terms for one digital product

🎧 BEYOND THE PAGE

Scan for Steve's unfiltered insights and implementation hacks in this chapter. (2-3 min)

Not the audiobook. Better.

CHAPTER 14:

THE MIC DROP

The Transformation Point

"Reading this book without taking action is like studying a map while dying of thirst next to a river. You now know exactly what to do. The only question is whether you have the guts to f***king do it."

THE ESSENTIALS

- You now have all the tools to build an Unsellable business
- The real test isn't knowledge but implementation, taking consistent action
- Your expertise is too valuable to remain trapped or undervalued
- Building an ecosystem requires courage and commitment, not perfection
- The ecosystem you build will create freedom, impact, and wealth simultaneously

CASE STUDY: MARK — THE DECISION THAT CHANGED EVERYTHING

Before: Mark had the expertise but lived in endless false starts, overthinking every move.

Turning Point: He followed the Unsellable system, no guesswork, just a complete path.

After:

- Closed $85k in pre-sales
- Built his first hybrid leadership program
- Finally launched with full confidence

"I didn't need another idea. I needed a complete system I could trust."

You made it.

Not just to the end of this book, but to the edge of the old you.

The version of you that:

- Waited for perfect
- Overthought the offer
- Got stuck in tech hell
- Panicked on sales calls
- Woke up with a gift but no game plan
- Doubted whether this was really going to work

That version?

They're done.

Because now?

You see it.

You see the ecosystem. You see the flywheel. You see the way forward that doesn't involve selling your time like a tradesperson or burning yourself out doing "value content" for an audience that never buys.

You see, the business that can only be built by you and, because of that, can never be taken from you.

And that, my friend, is what makes it UNSELLABLE.

THE POINT OF NO RETURN

There's something powerful that happens when you truly see a new possibility. You can never unsee it.

That's where you are now.

You've glimpsed what's possible when you:

- Stop trying to build a "normal business"
- Start building an ecosystem that leverages your genius
- Refuse to separate who you are from what you build

- Commit to creating something authentic and uncompromising
- Decide that your expertise is too valuable to be undervalued

This isn't just a new strategy. It's a new identity.

HERE'S WHAT YOU'VE LEARNED

You've learned how to:

- Identify if you're ready to play this game
- Package your genius into scalable formats
- Create a pricing model that reflects real value
- Protect your IP without turning into a paranoid hermit
- Stand up a tech stack that works while you rest
- Run marketing that makes you visible without selling your soul
- Close deals without feeling slimy
- Deliver results without burning out
- Build momentum without losing control

That's not a funnel. That's not a course. That's not a coaching program.

That's a movement.

And you're the engine behind it.

THE UNSELLABLE ARSENAL

Let's take inventory of the weapons you now have at your disposal:

Chapter	Core Lesson	Your New Power
1-3	You are the business	Confidence to build around your unique value
4-5	The Expert Ecosystem	A framework for leveraging what you know
6-7	Building strategically	The ability to create once, profit repeatedly
8-9	Tech & Marketing	Systems that work while you sleep
10-11	Sales & Pricing	The confidence to charge what you're worth
12-13	Scaling & Selling	Conversations that convert without compromise
14-15	Lifestyle & Protection	Freedom with security

WHAT HAPPENS NEXT IS UP TO YOU

Close this book and do nothing?

Fine. Stay clever, stay stuck.

But if you're ready to stop circling potential and start cashing in on proven profitable, purposeful impact...

Then here's what we've got for you:

Step 1: Take the Diagnostic: Scan the QR code. Answer the questions. Get your ecosystem score. Find your gaps. Choose your next cog.

Step 2: Join us: Become part of the Expert Incubator and the Learn Awesome Expert Community. Surround yourself with other real-deal experts building category-crushing businesses without selling out.

Step 3: Get The Operating System: This was the intro. ExpertOS Mini and Expert OS are your operating systems. Deep dives into all the cogs, how to build them, tools, templates, scripts, and a library of content to help you create. We're handing you the blueprint. Scan the QR code to check them out

Step 4: Attend one of our events: Sometimes it's just more practical to get in a room or a zoom session with likeminded experts and work with Steve to simply get your stuff done. There are regular in person or digital events running throughout the year. Scan the QR code to check them out.

THE DECISION POINT

This moment, right now, is a fork in the road:

Path One: Stay As You Are	Path Two: Build the Unsellable
Continue trading time for money	Build assets that work while you sleep
Keep undercharging for your expertise	Price based on the value you create
Remain at the mercy of client whims	Create a system that attracts the right clients
Hope for referrals and word of mouth	Build a marketing machine that never stops
Wonder if you'll ever break through	Know exactly how you'll scale and grow

There's no judgment here. Path One is comfortable. Familiar. Safe. Path Two requires courage. Commitment. Conviction.

But you wouldn't have read this far if you were satisfied with comfortable.

THE FINAL TRUTH

You don't need a new funnel. You don't need a new logo.

You need to stop pretending you don't already have what it takes.

You've got the skills. You've got the experience. You've got the results. You've got the stories.

You've got the fire.

Now you've got the plan.

So go.

Go build. Go sell. Go stand on stages. Go license your content. Go fix the problems that are costing companies millions. Go get paid what you're worth and provide the impact you were put here to provide.

Because Unsellable isn't just a business model.

It's a code. It's a mindset. It's a rejection of every shitty rule we've been taught about what success should look like.

And now?

You're proof that there's another way.

Let's build it together.

IMPLEMENTATION STEPS

ONE BIG THING: → Choose the ONE chapter from this book that addresses your most critical need and block 2 hours this week to complete its implementation steps.

Two Small Steps:

- Identify an accountability partner who will check in on your progress
- Set a 30-day goal that would meaningfully move your business toward the Unsellable model

BEYOND THE PAGE

Scan for Steve's unfiltered insights and implementation hacks in this chapter. (2-3 min)

Not the audiobook. Better.

www.ingramcontent.com/pod-product-compliance
Lightning Source LLC
Chambersburg PA
CBHW070959040426
42443CB00007B/571